INTERRUPTED to *BE*

Expanded Edition

A Shepherd Boy's Journey to Kingship

DR. ANNIE B. WILDER

Author of On the *Other Side of Bitter*

ABW
DR. ANNIE B. WILDER
PUBLISHING

ISBN: 978-1-963917-64-2 (paperback)
ISBN: 978-1-963917-66-6 (hardcover)
ISBN: 978-1-963917-65-9 (epub)

Library of Congress Control Number: 2026902886

CONTENTS

Preface

Personal prophecy is a spontaneous utterance inspired by the Holy Spirit and spoken by an individual for the purpose of edification, exhortation, and comfort. The *New Webster's Dictionary and Thesaurus* defines these words as follows: *Edify*—to build up, in a moral sense, to instruct or improve generally. *Exhort*—to urge to a good deed, to encourage, to warn. Comfort—to console, to gladden (1 Corinthians 14:3). Prophecy is a spiritual gift (1 Corinthians 12:10) to be desired (1 Corinthians 14:1) and is given in part (1 Corinthians 13:9). That means God reveals a portion of His plan for our lives at a time. Its fulfillment is a process that requires us to believe, obey, and exercise patience.

Therein is a problem for many individuals. What is meant to encourage, edify, and comfort can, when not understood, become a snare. Often the individuals receiving the prophecy expect its fulfillment to be immediate. Instead, it is intended for us to be encouraged in the state we are found. Sadly, so often it causes a different response. Many times an individual's response is one of paralysis and indecision. The recipient of the prophecy often spends years, and even the remainder of their lives, unable to live in the now for fear of missing what is to happen in the passage of time.

These individuals, using their own reasoning, constantly try to fashion their every move, or lack thereof, around the fulfillment of the prophecy. Others go about laying out their everyday functioning based on what they think the direction of the prophecy will take. Such behavior assumes God needs our help. God is the one to watch over the utterance to give it to be manifested He made this fact clear in Isaiah 55:11: "So is My Word that goes out from My mouth: It will not return to Me empty, but will accomplish what I desire and will achieve the purpose for which I sent it."

The plan is the Lord's. Many things will usually happen to bring about fulfillment of the prophecy. I repeat our part in the process requires faith, obedience, and patience. Oh, by the way, we can be assured that God will interrupt and redirect our self-selected plans in life to bring about the fulfillment of His plan.

Rather, most often these situations are all about preparing you for fulfillment of your purpose. They may actually be about sharpening those Godly traits placed in you when you were conceived in your mother's womb. Furthermore, the circumstances you now find yourself could be to expose you to people and places that are part of your destiny. On the other hand, it maybe for exposing something within you—a tightly concealed snare devised by the enemy for your demise. We are not to be ignorant of the enemy's devices.

These principles will be demonstrated in this book through the early life of David. He is known by some as King David and others as David the giant slayer. This part of his life begins in 1 Samuel 16:1 and goes through to 2 Samuel 6. He was a lad when he had been chosen by God to become the next king over Israel. However, he was thirty-three years old when he was anointed for partial fulfillment of his destiny. It would be another seven and half years before being anointed to completely embrace the fulfillment of God's plan for His life.

We will see that David suffered rejection, experienced being accused of performing activities for the wrong motives, was returned wrong for his good deeds, and was chased out of his homeland. These were all after God had chosen him to be the next king of the great nation of Israel. David did not become immobile, paralyzed, or inactive. Fulfillment of his destiny was not to take place on the sidelines. It was to take place in the process of time as he navigated through each of these life encounters. Most often the delay, or lack of activity, currently being experienced is preparation time for something beyond our imagination. Sometimes it is to bring to pass that God-inspired thing that we dare to imagine. My confidence regarding these facts comes from observations and conversations with friends, clients, and personal experiences.

Acknowledgments

Honor, glory, and praise to God for this completed assignment.

For whatsoever things were written aforetime were written for our learning, that we through patience and comfort of the scriptures might have hope.

—Romans 15:4

ENDORSEMENTS

I have read the original publication of *Interrupted to BE* many times since 2016, and each reading continues to bring new insight and encouragement to my life. The book's twists, turns, and mysteries—both in David's story and our own—are revealed to have purpose. It teaches patience, obedience, and trust during uncertain seasons, guiding readers to embrace God's perfect timing and greater purpose when life interrupts the path we are on.

— G.S.

"The man who does the will of God lives forever." —1 John 2:17 Interrupted to BE beautifully illustrates that God's will is always rooted in divine love and growth beyond our expectations. Dr. Wilder's portrayal of David's journey offers powerful insight into listening, waiting, and finding value in life's trials. Through her masterful application of biblical principles to modern life, this book becomes a treasured resource for understanding how God uses every experience for our good and His glory, equipping readers to live a fulfilled, faith-centered life.

— Bob S.

Interrupted to Be: Expanded Edition is an inspiring work that affirms the power of purpose, faith, and growth through life's interruptions. The message resonates clearly, offering meaningful insight that encourages readers to trust the process and embrace divine direction even in uncertain seasons.

— SeaAmos Business Solutions

Introduction

Why can't things just go as planned? This is a question practically everybody has asked at one time or another in life. Whether referring to romantic relationships, employment, educational pursuits, or having to suddenly deplete savings to cover unexpected expenses, the question has been raised. The very fact that the question is posed indicates a level of frustration, bewilderment, and oftentimes anger. The underlying reason for the question is often the result of plans we thought we had control over suddenly being out of our control. The matter is further complicated by the fact that we are left without knowledge of what caused our plans to stray off course. Depending on how determined we are in doing things as we planned, the situation can throw us into a crisis situation.

The dictionary defines interruption as "the act of breaking into the progress of,"— "obstruction or hindrance,"— "cause of stoppage." I like "breaking into the progress of." The word be is defined by the same source as "exist," "occur," or "take place." Putting the two together, we derive the focus of this book title.

INTERRUPTED to *BE*

is a breaking into the progress of an existing action or process to prepare for another to take place.

That definition describes "life." The one sure thing about "life" is it just doesn't unfold in a predictable manner. Yes, we lay out great plans for our lives, and to some degree, we are able to follow those plans. But so often they get interrupted. When that happens, we are tossed on to a course in life never dreamed or imagined. That is not always a bad thing. In fact, it can be an exciting journey resulting in self — enrichment, personal and spiritual growth, empowerment, and even promotion.

One concept that is difficult for us to grasp is that interruptions are sometimes God's doing—for our good. Sometimes they are simply permitted by Him—also for our ultimate good. Great, but do we know this fact at the time? Unfortunately, we don't. The one thing that is usually certain is that the prior enjoyable experience has now given way to high levels of stress, anxiety, uncertainty, and often the question that is repeated over and over and over again: *Why?*

I am so very excited that the Lord has enabled me to pen this book. My prayer is that it will help the many who operate in a continuous state of stress and anxiety because of sudden interruptions in life. It is also to help others put the periods of unproductive activities, or seeming lack of activities, in their lives in perspective. What you are experiencing isn't that God has forgotten you. It isn't that the prophecies that have been spoken over you were of a false prophet. It isn't even that your time has come and gone or that you are the only person in life without a God-given purpose.

Rather, most often these situations are all about preparing you for fulfillment of your purpose. They may actually be about sharpening those Godly traits placed in you when you were conceived in your mother's womb. Furthermore, the circumstances you now find yourself could be to expose you to people and places that are part of your destiny. On the other hand, it maybe for exposing something within you—a tightly concealed snare devised by the enemy for your demise. We are not to be ignorant of the enemy's devices.

These principles will be demonstrated in this book through the early life of David. He is known by some as King David and others as David the giant slayer. This part of his life begins in 1 Samuel 16:1 and goes through to 2 Samuel 6. He was a lad when he had been chosen by God to become the next king over Israel. However, he was thirty-three years old when he was anointed for partial fulfillment of his destiny. It would be another seven and half years before being anointed to completely embrace the fulfillment of God's plan for His life.

We will see that David suffered rejection, experienced being accused of performing activities for the wrong motives, was returned wrong for his good deeds, and was chased out of his homeland. These were all after God had chosen him to be the next king of the great nation of Israel. David did not become immobile, paralyzed, or inactive. Fulfillment of his destiny was not to take place on the sidelines. It was to take place in the process of time as he navigated through each of these life encounters. Most often the delay, or lack of activity, currently being experienced is preparation time for something beyond our imagination. Sometimes it is to bring to pass that God-inspired thing that we dare to imagine. My confidence regarding these facts comes from observations and conversations with friends, clients, and personal experiences.

A man's heart deviseth his way: but the Lord directeth his steps.

—Proverbs 16:9

CHAPTER 1

A Heart Condition Left Unattended
1 Samuel 15:1 — 35

The nation of Israel had come through a time of total dependence upon the Lord. God had given them victories through the leadership of various individuals in the office of judge. The time of judges folded into leadership through individuals in the office of prophet. Samuel, an individual that had spent all his days in the temple of the Lord, was the last of the judges and the first to occupy the office of prophet. He was not the first prophet but the first to occupy that office. Through his spiritual leadership and obedience to God, the nation of Israel had experienced many victories in battle.

The nation of Israel now insisted that they be given an earthly king to reign over them. Their desire was based on nothing more than wanting to be like the nations round about them. They wanted a king that would go out before them and fight their battles. That was not God's desire for them. However, because of their insistence, God gave them what they wanted. He granted their request and gave them an individual to serve as their king.

The name of this individual was Saul. He was tall and handsome. His appearance fit the nations' expectations of a warrior. He began his reign with the qualities of a leader: humility. restraint, Godly concern, wisdom, and praise. However, he also had character flaws which might have been concealed by his positive qualities. The most troublesome of these were disobedience and hypocrisy. These were deep-rooted issues hidden in his heart. Eventually, they surfaced and caused him much trouble. On multiple occasions, Saul disobeyed the commands of God without immediate consequences. However, his problem of disobedience reached its summit when he failed to carry out a detailed assignment. Specifically, he was told to destroy-totally destroy-a historic enemy of the nation, along with everything in that city the king, livestock, and all. Instead, Saul returned home from battle with the king and the best of the livestock. Later, the prophet Samuel confronted him regarding his actions. He compounded his sin of disobedience by blaming the people for his decision to disobey God.

1

Twofold Consequences

The consequences of his disobedience were tragic and twofold. The firstved from the position of king immediately. What would happen shortly would be the withdrawal of God's supernatural empowerment (anointing) for the office. Once God's anointing was withdrawn, Saul would no longer able to receive direction from God and help that ensured victories in battle. He would not personally experience that privilege again.

The second consequence of his deliberate disobedience was a broken fellowship with God. Saul himself was not rejected by God. It was his personal relationship with God that was affected. His sins would cause the Lord not to hear his prayers (Isaiah 59:2). However, restoration of his fellowship with God was possible. Whether or not he would receive restoration would be contingent solely upon what he would do next.

Saul needed to sincerely repent for his disobedience. Indeed, it appeared that he was sorry for his actions. He had said to Samuel, "I have sinned: for I have transgressed the commandment of the Lord, and thy words: because I feared the people, and obeyed their voice" (1 Samuel 15:24). He then pleaded with Samuel the prophet to stand with him before the people. Was his sorrow that of Godly sorrow that brings repentance, or was it sorrow due to the loss of position? His words revealed that his outward act of repentance was not based on a heartfelt sorrow resulting from Almighty God's displeasure toward him. His concern was that of maintaining his image before the people. His heart was not broken before God. His spirit was not contrite (oppressed by the burden of sin and desired freedom from its enslavement).

Lost Kingship versus Broken Fellowship

Saul was rejected from reigning as king, but he himself was not rejected. These are two distinctively different issues. They may seem the same, but they are not. The consequences of being rejected as king meant he would not receive God's help and protection in warfare against the enemies of the land. Broken fellowship with God would leave him personally void of the protective care of the Lord. That is a frightening place to be found. It is a place of vulnerability and susceptibility to enemy attacks and overtaking.

Evidence of Emotional Instability

Already, in times past, Saul had bouts of what might be described as emotional instability. On one occasion, he had strictly forbidden his warring men to eat while engaged in battle. During times of battle would be the time that their strength was greatly needed. In the second year of his reign as king, he had also disobeyed another of God's commands. He had been told to await the arrival of Samuel to give further military instructions regarding an impending battle against the Philistines. The prophet's arrival was delayed. Saul's army of men became fearful and began to scatter. The Philistine army gathered nearby, and God had not given him instructions, so he took it upon himself to make the sacrifice unto the Lord (1 Samuel 13:8-12). It was a duty reserved for priests. Saul was not a priest. Therefore, such an act was forbidden. On another occasion, he planned to kill his own son for failing to obey a command for which his son had no knowledge.

What Was Then Is Now

The situation Saul found himself is far too common in our society today. Sometimes the root of the problem is a known sin. Oftentimes the problem is a weight described as unnecessary baggage, hindrance, or encumbrance. It would include anything that we give excessive affection that draws us away from Godly principles. The twelfth chapter of Hebrews warns us to also attend to any weights we might be carrying. That is because a weight left unattended could result in sin. Sin or weight, they must be put off. The potential consequences of either are extremely serious, so serious, in fact, that God often interrupts our lives to allow situations that will reveal these areas to arise.

Many times these interruptions come as a thief in the night-unannounced and totally unexpected! They are not usually recognized as intended for good. Oftentimes such interruptions in our lives come before being launched into positions of added responsibility. Sometimes they come to curtail further deterioration in an existing faltering situation. How awesome that God is so vested in our succeeding in life that He pulls us aside to address issues that are or could interfere with our ability to embrace the life Jesus came to provide for us—life and that more abundantly—personally,professionally, spiritually, relationally, and emotionally. What must be noted is what happened with Saul was due to a condition of his heart. It was a condition that was left unattended.

Point to Ponder – Condition Left Unattended

Saul's story reminds us that outward appearance and initial success cannot cover a heart that is not aligned with God. Left unchecked, disobedience, pride, and compromise can lead to missed opportunities, broken fellowship, and vulnerability to life's attacks. True success begins in the heart—attending to it daily through obedience, humility, and repentance. Let us examine our own hearts and surrender every hidden flaw to God, for He values a contrite heart more than outward performance.

CHAPTER 2

A Replacement Identified
1 Samuel 16:1 — 13

God's rejection of Saul as king required the appointment of his replacement. God told Samuel He had chosen a man after His own heart for the position. He was not told the name of the person. God only told Samuel that He would make the replacement known to him. Samuel's immediate instructions were to journey to the house of man named Jesse. There, he was to conduct a ceremony announced as a sacrifice unto the Lord. The prophet Samuel had been given the command to perform the anointing in this manner to keep it concealed from Saul. If Saul had known, he might have killed Samuel.

During this private ceremony, Jesse had all of his eight sons present, except the youngest. The youngest was out in the pastures watching the sheep. Of course, Samuel was unaware of this fact. He had only been told (1) to go there with his horn of oil, (2) to announce a sacrifice to the Lord and call Jesse to it, that (3) God's choice for the next king would be there, and that (4) he was to anoint unto God the individual God would identify.

The ceremony followed a course of action that would have given Samuel to anoint Jesse's eldest son. His choice was based on the son's outward appearance and height. However, God stopped him by saying, "Man looks at the outward appearance, but God looks at the heart." The other six sons proceeded to pass before Samuel without God at any point making choice of any of them. Puzzled that God had not given him instructions to anoint any of them, the prophet Samuel asked Jesse, "Are these all the sons you have?" It was then that Jesse informed Samuel of the fact that his youngest son was out watching the sheep. Jesse was instructed to summon this son from the pastures. The ceremony would not continue until he arrived.

The Ceremony Proceeds

Upon arrival of Jesse's youngest son from the pastures, the Lord said to Samuel, "Anoint him, he is the one." God had chosen the youngest of Jesse's eight boys to reign as the king of the united kingdom of Israel. This lad was a teenager by the name of David. The prophet Samuel took his horn of oil and poured it upon the lad in the presence of his brothers. This action called anointing was symbolic of an inward work taking place in the lad. God, at that time, transferred His spirit from King Saul to David. It was this supernatural impartation that had enabled Saul to succeed in battle. David now possessed it while King Saul was left in the position of king but void.

A Man after God's Heart

There have been many conjectures as to what gave David the distinction of being a man after God's heart. The answer was revealed to me as I also pondered this matter. He had been gifted with the willingness to do everything God wanted him to do (Acts 13:22). It would be during his life's journey of experiences that the characteristics of this gift would come to the surface, be matured and utilized to make an impact to the lives of a great number of people. It was the purpose of the journey.

It Happened Before

It was like other examples throughout Scripture where God spoke the end at the beginning. One of the most outstanding of these accounts is found in the sixth chapter of Judges. There, we find the journey of an individual named Gideon as he developed into the man God had created him to be. The angel of the Lord appeared to him and addressed him as a mighty man of valor—a mighty man of valor! The definition of the word (valor) indicates that Gideon was a man of courage and bravery. That is the way God saw him. However, Gideon, at that time, had no such outward characteristic. In fact, the angel found him preparing wheat away from the customary place for fear of being discovered. His response to the angel was also that of doubt and disbelief. He was questioning the reports regarding the wonders God had performed in the lives of his ancestors. He even accused God of having abandoned them. regarding the wonders God had performed in the lives of his ancestors. He even accused God of having abandoned them.

God was addressing Gideon based on who and what He had created him to become. Therefore, He wasn't moved because of Gideon's questions, doubts, and disbelief. In fact, God followed up His initial greeting by informing Gideon of the assignment that would demonstrate this calling. He would be the instrument through which God would rescue His nation from the hands of their enemy, the Midianites. At that point, Gideon began asking for proof by way of a sign that he was speaking to God. Upon receiving the proof he was seeking, he became gravely afraid— "I have seen the angel of God face to face!"

A Fearful Heart Settled

God told Gideon not to be afraid and that he was not going to die. Through a series of experiences, God began working in Gideon's life to develop him into the person he was called to be. Involved were instances that gave Gideon to know that God being with him was all he needed to provide the nation victory. There were also situations to demonstrate that God would perform the battle. He was fully prepared when the hour came for him to perform the task in which he was beforetime appointed. God had walked him through numerous experiences and situations designed to perfect the potential instilled in him before birth. His later days had no resemblance of his earlier days of hiding for fear of his nation's enemy. He became that mighty man of valor God addressed before he could imagine such a personal distinction.

Likewise would it be for David. When anointed, he had the potential within him of demonstrating a heart after God's. Now God would provide circumstances through which his willingness to do what God wanted would come to the forefront. He would not mount the throne at this time. He was anointed but not yet to be appointed. His journey from the sheep pasture to the king's palace would meet with many interruptions along the way. However, none of his experiences would be wasted. They would all contribute to the fulfillment of his God-destined purpose.

Point to Ponder

A man after God's own heart is one whose deepest desire is to do the will of God — a person who may stumhivine direction.

CHAPTER 3

The Rejected Meets the Chosen
1 Samuel 16:14 — 23

King Saul's disobedience and rejection of the word of God resulted in God withdrawing His spirit and enabling power for battle from him. However, it also had more far-reaching consequences. Our text tells us, "An evil spirit from the Lord troubled him." For clarity, it must be noted this expression is a Hebrew idiom. The expression cannot be understood from the separate words but the language of the culture. The belief was that all good and evil was God's doing. In fact, the evil spirit was not sent by the Lord. Rather, what happened to Saul is an example of the potential danger facing anyone that continues to deliberately disobey the Lord. Saul's multiple instances of disobedience and outright rejection of God's instructions resulted in God's protective shield being removed from him. Thereby, the evil spirit had permission (not directed) to buffet him. In the passage of time, Saul would experience the full-blown assault of this evil spirit.

Ungodly Counsel

"Blessed is the man that walketh not in the counsel of the ungodly" (Psalm 1:1). Sadly, the individuals Saul held close to him and from whom he received counsel were void of Godly wisdom or insight. Upon observing Saul being troubled by this evil spirit, his servants suggested getting a cunning player on the harp to play for him at these times. They suggested to the king that he would feel better with the playing of the harp. One of the king's servants told the king he had seen the son of one of the nearby sheepherders that was not only cunning in playing, but was also a mighty valiant man, a man of war, prudent in matters, a comely person with the Lord on his side. It is not clear as to the reason the servants felt to add all these characteristics regarding David at this time. The question is, why would they say such things about him?

My Personal Insight

I am personally aware of the fact that other individuals can often see latent gifts and hidden potentials in our lives long before they come to maturity. The command given to parents to train their children in the way they should go supports this fact. All individuals are born with a unique temperament (inborn traits) that, if noticed, should be nurtured. Some children demonstrate leadership capabilities early; some display musical talents, motivational skills, and entrepreneurial tendencies. Of course, these are only a few of the nearly endless number of character traits. go supports this fact. All individuals are born with a unique temperament (inborn traits) that, if noticed, should be nurtured. Some children demonstrate leadership capabilities early; some display musical talents, motivational skills, and entrepreneurial tendencies. Of course, these are only a few of the nearly endless number of character traits.

God had warned the nation that the king they insisted on having over them would take for his personal use men that he saw as being strong and valiant (1 Samuel 8:11). Indeed, this had been characteristic of King Saul. I suggest that his servants were keenly aware of this fact. Therefore, I surmise that the servant was decreeing the added attributes to ensure the king's approval.

A Pleasing Sound

The words of the servant were indeed pleasing to King Saul, so he sent messengers to David's dad, saying, "Send me David, your son." David arrived, and King Saul loved him and appointed him as his armor bearer. He also sent word back to David's father, saying, "Let David stand before me." Furthermore, he informed Jesse, David's father, that David had found favor with him. The occasion came that the evil spirit came upon King Saul. Just as his servants had suggested, David played the harp, and the king was helped.

Very much like life today. People will do almost anything, except the one thing that is required to experience true deliverance and healing: more drugs, more alcohol, more relationships, experimental sexual activities, job changes, more cars, bigger houses. The list goes on and on. Saul had a heart condition that music could not cure. The best help he could get from following the counsel of his servants was temporary relief.

Wise Counsel

In the multitude of counselors, there is safety, and many people love to give advice. Therefore, we must be careful as to whom we take counsel from. We should question the source of the advice individuals are offering. Is it from their selfish desired outcome, or is it intended to draw our attention back into obedience to the word of God?

Furthermore, Scripture forewarns us that the time will come when sound doctrine will not be endured. Instead, many individuals will draw to themselves teachers that appeal to their selfish desires. King Saul needed to acknowledge he had a problem. He then needed to want to be set free. He needed to commit to working at being better rather than temporarily feeling better. That would have been the focus of a wise counselor rather than using flattering words to appease.

The approach a wise counselor might have used to reason with King Saul are yet offered to anyone currently experiencing hurt due to calamities, afflictions in life, or the burden of sin. Freedom from such slavery is available. Saul had rejected earlier counsel from the Godly prophet Samuel, so we might conclude that he could only hear that which appealed to his desires. His self-seeking or just plain unwise counselors accommodated him. Amazingly, their counsel provided for the rejected (Saul) to meet the chosen (David).

Point to Ponder

Life often tempts us to settle for quick fixes—short-lived relief from pain, fear, or stress. Like King Saul, we may seek comfort in temporary solutions that soothe but do not heal the heart. True deliverance and lasting healing come not from human ingenuity or fleeting pleasures but from God's intervention and obedience to His Word. David's music brought Saul a momentary reprieve, yet the ultimate solution would have been full alignment with God. Let us remember: temporary relief may calm the storm, but only God's power and guidance provide complete and enduring restoration.

CHAPTER 4

Enemies Within, Enemies Without
1 Samuel 17:1 — 58

When Saul and his army of men went out to battle, David returned to his duties of caring for his father's sheep. His time in the palace was interrupted because of the battle. One day his father called upon him to carry provisions to his three elder brothers out on the battlefield. He was sent to check on how the battle was going. David arrived to find much fear in the camp due to the taunting of a Philistine giant by the name of Goliath. Saul and his army of men were gripped with fear of the Philistine giant.

This Is All Wrong

David's response was quite the opposite. He was appalled at what he was seeing and hearing an enemy of Israel would dare show himself with such defiance! David asked, "For who is this uncircumcised Philistine that he should defy the armies of the living God?" The scene was all wrong, and somebody needed to do something. It was obvious that he should be that somebody. David's journey thus far in life had prepared him for such a time as this. Courage was needed—David had courage. The ability to recognize whose battle was to be fought—David knew this was the Lord's battle. A keen sense of the location of the enemy was required. David was able to distinguish the direction from which his enemy would approach. The character traits already lodged in him would provide for many victories to be won in his lifetime, beginning right there in the camp.

Enemies from Within

His first victory came as he defeated his first enemy within the camp. His brother greeted him upon his arrival with the provisions from his father by saying, "With whom have you left those few sheep?" Those few sheep—had his role in the family been seen as small and menial? His brother added, "I know your pride and naughtiness of heart." He now presumed to know

David's motive for appearing there. None of these things moved David. He simply replied, "Is there not a cause?" He knew he had come in obedience to his father. Therefore, he would not entertain such negative accusations. He did not allow his brother's demeaning remarks to discourage him. In fact, it would soon be evident that it was such a time as this that David had appeared on the scene. demeaning remarks to discourage him. In fact, it would soon be evident that it was such a time as this that David had appeared on thescene. demeaning remarks to discourage him. In fact, it would soon be evident that it was such a time as this that David had appeared on the scene.

The next enemy to be confronted within the camp was that of being judged because of his age. King Saul made an uninformed assessment of David's warfare capabilities. He could only see that David was young. He was unaware of the fact that time in the field with the sheep had required David to engage in warfare. David, like many of us, had had experiences in life maybe earlier than he should. David's was the responsibility of the sheep—many of ours might have been the care of siblings while being but a child ourselves. Even worse, it might be because of the need to take on the role of the adult in the family because the adults are incapacitated because of illness, an addiction, or the parents' work schedule. I certainly can relate to such a situation when growing up. In fact, I yet cry these many years later each time I recall the day my dad came and pulled me out of school, took me home, and beat (yes, beat) me because the babysitter didn't show up and my siblings had been left alone.

David did not become discouraged and disheartened. He simply informed the king of his prior successes. He told the king of an incident that required him to slay both a lion and bear to recover a sheep taken from his father's herd. He concluded the matter by telling the king that the Lord had delivered him before and would do it again.

There was also a third enemy within the camp. This one centered on the weaponry to be used. Saul wanted David to wear his military attire. David, in obedience, attempted to wear it. However, he soon had to let the king know it would not work for him. He said, "I have not proved them. He then pulled them off (1 Samuel 17:39). David had not tested the customary battle armor, but his trust in God had been tried and proven to be reliable. The source of his help had become evident to him long before this situation.

It had happened while in the solitary surroundings of sheep.

Enemy Outside the Camp

Finally, David was ready to face the enemy outside the camp. He sized up the opponent and came to the conclusion that Goliath, the lion, and the bear were the same size with God. His confidence was not in himself. It rested in the faithfulness of the God who had helped him many times before. David stated the key to his confidence: "The God that delivered me out of the paw of the lion and out of the paw of the bear, He will deliver me out of the hand of this Philistine" (1 Samuel 17:37). He was confident in the God that had proven Himself mightier than any enemy he had encountered while in the field with the sheep. That confidence proved he had the courage required for this task. He was not intimidated by the physical size of this opponent. The taunting words of this giant didn't move him. The tools David had in his possession throughout his time in the field included a shepherd's bag and a slingshot. During his time in the field, these had been the tools through which God had given him victory. He had no doubts that the God that was with him in the desolate pastures would be with him on the battlefield against Goliath. He was equipped with everything he needed to be victorious.

A Mighty Victory

David's unwavering faith, courage, and confidence in God were rewarded. He defeated the giant and gained the favor of the king. The course of his life would undergo change again. Saul bought David back to the palace. King Saul's son, Jonathan, loved him, and their hearts became knitted together. Saul also made David captain of his army. He would never again return to watching his father Jesse's sheep.

Personally, I've learned that what we consider delay or being forgotten is often quite the contrary—it has purpose. Specifically, I'm learning more and more to take inventory of what I have rather than what I think I need and do not have. Time and time again, I have enjoyed the fruit of trusting the fact that if God has given me a task, He has already equipped me to perform it.

Point to Ponder

The greatest battles are often won long before we face the giant—won in hidden places, through quiet faithfulness, small victories, and trust in God's past deliverance. Before defeating the enemy outside, we must first conquer the doubts, voices, and fears within. What God has already placed in your hands is enough for the victory He has called you to.

CHAPTER 5

A Sad Situation
1 Samuel 18:1 — 30

Davis avid was now promoted, so to say, from his prior position of shepherd boy. He would no longer be spending the long summer days and cold winter nights in the pastures with the sheep, making the long trek up the mountains through the valleys to spend the summers where there was good grazing for the sheep, then down to escape the approaching winter snow. Anointed and destined to be the next king, he would have the luxuries that came with the position, so we would think. He was anointed for the position of king, but he had not been placed in the position. He was, however, in the palace in close relationship with the reigning king. It seems this would have been the perfect place for David to be groomed for kingship. However, that would not be the case. In fact, enjoyment of such luxuries would be short-lived.

Remember, David had been brought to the palace to play the harp for King Saul because he would be bothered by an evil spirit. Now David was going out to war. He was accepted in the sight of the people of Israel and by Saul's servants. Additionally, women would greet the army of men upon returning from battle with victory songs. The problem was that they gave greater numbers of victories to David than to Saul. What triggered the evil spirit to manifest in Saul prior to this? It is not known. Now the catalyst seemed to be the songs and popularity that David was receiving. These things might have given Saul to remember what Samuel the prophet had told him earlier: "The Lord has torn the kingdom of Israel from you today and has given it to one of your neighbors—to one better than you" (1 Samuel 15:28).

Seeing David's popularity and mighty exploits made Saul think, what else is there for David but the kingdom? From that day forward, Saul began to see David differently. The thoughts of his heart were exposed the next morning. Once again, he had come under the attack of the evil spirit. While David played for him as in times past, Saul cast a javelin he held in his hand at David. He intended to kill him. In fact, he tried twice, and twice,

David escaped. One failed attempt to destroy David would not stop Saul. He would simply try a different tactic. However, he feared the people because they loved David.

Therefore, Saul reasoned that he would destroy David in a manner that would place the blame elsewhere. Saul's first tactic involved offering David to become his son-in-law in exchange for one hundred foreskins of the Philistines as a dowry. The actual intent was that David would be killed by the Philistines while attempting to obtain the foreskins. David accepted the challenge and returned with twice as many foreskins.

David's safe return caused Saul to be enraged the more. It was then that Saul realized that the spirit of God had departed from his life and was now with David. That realization caused him to now fear David. It also caused him to be driven by the evil spirit—he was out of control. The evil spirit was now in full-blown mode. Saul would be David's enemy from this point forward.

Point to Ponder

Not every promotion leads to peace, and not every open door is free of opposition. Sometimes God's favor on your life will provoke jealousy in others—but their actions cannot cancel God's plan. When the enemy rises against you, remember: the presence of God with you is greater than the hostility around you.

CHAPTER 6

Letting Go Is Hard to Do
1 Samuel 19:1 — 24

One of the first teachings in domestic violence groups that victims of abuse receive is that of the cycle of domestic violence. It is a three-phase diagram using arrows to make a circle and labeled phase 1 (tension building), phase 2 (acute battering incident), and phase 3 (honeymoon). It is a very effective means of depicting the progression that usually occurs in an abusive relationship. The troublesome phase of the cycle is that of the honeymoon phase because it is extremely deceiving. It is sandwiched between an explosive episode and the escalation of emotions that often leads to another explosive episode. During the honeymoon phase, the abuser often gives halfhearted apologies and promises to change. Those words are often a trap to lure the victim back into the relationship. The victim falls into the trap because the promise to change gives them a glimpse of the person they fell in love with and hopes of the dreamed life and love they so desperately desire.

David Returns

Such might have been the case with David. Saul next commanded his son and all his servants to kill David, but Jonathan reasoned with him on David's behalf. He reminded his father of how David had put his own life in danger to accomplish great victories for Israel. Jonathan further reminded him of the fact that he too had rejoiced over the victories accomplished by David. At Jonathan's insistence, Saul pulled back and promised he would not harm David. Like abuse victims during the honeymoon stage, Jonathan believed his father and rushed off to bring David back. David, once again, returned to duties in Saul's service. These included fighting against the Philistines whenever war would break out. Each time he would return from the battle with victory because the Lord was with him.

The diagram is called a cycle because that is exactly what it is. In a predictable manner, one phase follows the other again and again. Movement from one phase to the other happens faster and faster. It also grows worse, not because true change is impossible, but most often the abuser has not attended to the underlying problem and the victim has not accepted the reality of the situation. Following this same pattern, Saul's anger had grown worse than ever before. Once again, David stood playing the harp to soothe the evil spirit that tormented Saul. Again, Saul launched his javelin at David in an attempt to kill him. Again as in times past, David managed to dodge the javelin and escape. His respite had been short-lived.

Saul was now more determined than ever to kill David. His promise to Jonathan was null and void. He dispatched messengers to David's house with instructions to watch him through the night and kill him in the morning. Being aware of her father's new plot, Michal, David's wife, said to David, "If you don't run for your life tonight, tomorrow you will be killed." Often there are signs to let us know it is time to let go of a situation or relationship. It becomes obvious that it is either not right for us or that our time in a certain place has expired. However, for various reasons, in life, we make attempt after attempt to hold on in hopes of a different outcome. I imagine this must have been the situation with David. Otherwise, why would his wife, Saul's daughter Michael, need to speak so strongly to him?

Evidently, David needed a reality check. Michael's strong admonition was what he needed. He allowed his wife to help him escape. Meanwhile, she delayed the discovery of his escape by telling her father's messengers David was in bed sick. His response to their report was to bring him in his bed. He would kill him there. Returning to David's house to carry out the orders of the king, the messengers discovered that David was gone. The news caused Saul to verbally attack his daughter with accusations of deceiving him and assisting his enemy to escape. The evil spirit was driving Saul. need to speak so strongly to him?

Evidently, David needed a reality check. Michael's strong admonition was what he needed. He allowed his wife to help him escape. Meanwhile, she delayed the discovery of his escape by telling her father's messengers David was in bed sick. His response to their report was to bring him in his bed. He would kill him there. Returning to David's house to carry out the orders of the king, the messengers discovered that David was gone. The news caused Saul to verbally attack his daughter with accusations of deceiving him and assisting his enemy to escape. The evil spirit was driving Saul.

Point to Ponder

Sometimes the hardest part of growth is accepting when a season or relationship must end. God often provides clear signs, but we must have the courage to let go. Protection and purpose are found not in holding on, but in trusting God enough to walk away when He says it's time.

CHAPTER 7

An Unbelievable Situation
1 Samuel 20:1 — 42

Meanwhile, David was honestly confused about the matter. He appealed to Jonathan for answers. He asked, "What have I done? What is mine iniquity? What is my sin before your father that he seeks my life?" David wanted understanding, but the person he thought could explain was unable to do so at this time. Jonathan did not believe his father intended to do such a thing. He loved David, but he simply could not let himself believe this saying about his father.

Jonathan was blinded because he trusted his father. He believed his father was a man of his word. His father had said to him earlier regarding David, "As the Lord lives, he shall not be slain" (1 Samuel 19:6b). Jonathan was certain his father would not withhold any evil intentions of his heart regarding David. He had promised. Sadly, he was oblivious to the wickedness that lurked in his father's heart. Jonathan believed the relationship between he and his father was one of openness and honesty. He said to David, "My father will do nothing great or small without telling me. And why should my father hide this thing from me? It is not so!"

Jonathan was not able to answer David's questions, but David was able to give Jonathan a response to his question. David said to Jonathan, "Because your father knows how you feel towards me. He knows if he revealed his evil intent toward me you would be deeply hurt. Therefore, he has intentionally withheld this information from you."

David had finally accepted the fact that death was near for him at the hands of Saul if he tarried in the area. However, he was willing to risk remaining hidden in the area a few days longer to allow Jonathan time to personally investigate the matter. David would not return with Jonathan to the palace. Instead, they agreed that Jonathan would return and report having given David permission to return to his father's house for a gathering should his absence be questioned. Saul's response would do for Jonathan what Michal's strong admonition had done for David earlier. Indeed, the inquiry came, and Jonathan responded as he and David had agreed. Saul exploded and issued forth a string of verbally belittling and accusatory accusations. His actions confirmed David's report. "Send and fetch David to me for he shall surely die," Saul demanded. The heightened contempt raging within Saul would not allow him to verbally respond to Jonathan's questions, "Why should he be slain? What has he done?" Once again Saul was driven by the evil spirit. Instead of answering Jonathan, he cast a javelin at him as he had toward David. That act left no doubt in the mind of Jonathan. David's life was in danger.

Again, the duration of his time with the king in the palace was interrupted. Previously, it was because of a call to the battlefield. Now it was because of his need to remove himself from the threat of personal danger. David had performed every task assigned to him with excellence. His motive behind every action had been to bring victories to Israel in support and obedience to the king's instructions, as well as utilize his gift of music to abate the torment imposed on the king by the evil spirit. Our reasoning would be that these were all things that should have endeared David to Saul more. However, it was not to be. The reason was still unknown to David. But it was clear to both David and Jonathan he could not remain there. He needed to run for his life. In time, it would become clear that this was only one of many interruptions in his life orchestrated for a purpose.

Point to Ponder

There are moments in life when even those closest to us cannot see the truth we are facing. Yet God, in His wisdom, reveals what we need to know and when we need to know it. When circumstances force you to move on, trust that every interruption is part of His greater purpose-and a step toward where He is leading you next.

CHAPTER 8

Reasons beyond Expectation
1 Samuel 21:1 — 9

The word *El-Shaddai* is a characteristic of God that means "all-sufficient," "more than enough." The latter part of the definition really tickles me in situations orchestrated by the Lord in my life—that is time and time again, I am directed in some manner to perform or become engaged in an activity expecting a particular outcome. Either immediately or thereafter, I realize my steps were ordered in such a manner as to provide benefits beyond my expectation. It seldom turns out to be the way we think when the Lord is directing our steps.

I will share this one incident to explain what I mean. In the late 1990s, I returned to the University of New Haven to broaden my understanding of human behavior—to enhance my ministry—so I thought. For several semesters, I enjoyed the studies without thoughts of getting a degree. However, the time came that graduation was in view. A requirement for that completion was to do an internship which took place at a women's center. Again, my thoughts were that my actions were for my personal enrichment as opposed to another career. As it turned out, God was preparing me for another career and be the catalyst through which He would answer many prayers. I have now been there for more than ten years.

It seems David's circumstances were much the same. On the surface, it appeared that David was bought to the palace for Saul's sake. Actually, it was more to fulfill God's plan in David's development. The stage was being set for David to ascend to the office of his calling—the position he had been anointed. His true purpose for being in the palace at this time had multiple purposes.

For Israel's Sake

While he was hidden away in the pastures with the sheep, he was an unknown. By way of coming to the palace to play the harp for Saul, the nation of Israel had come to know him. Saul had become king because the people had specifically asked for someone to go out before them—a warrior. Now, by way of David coming to the palace to play for Saul and being placed in position as leader of the army, the people now knew him to be a capable warrior.

A Glimpse for David

David's life had been spent in the pastures. He probably felt that was where he was destined to spend the rest of his life. He needed his vision to be widened. He needed a glimpse into the world in which he was to become involved. He was not the only person God has done this for either before or after him. Joseph, with the coat of many colors, had gotten this glimpse in a dream (Genesis 37:1 — 11). Isaiah, in the Old Testament, had gotten his by way of a vision (Isaiah 6:1). Paul, in the New Testament, had gotten his by way of a drastic experience while en route to persecute the disciples of the Lord (Acts 9:1 — 31). But David was privileged to actually visit the place of his destiny. The first time, he would spend time close to the king. There, he would get to personally see up close the privileges rendered to the king. The second time was to experience the vast outer workings of the king—as warrior.

A Desolate Plight

The situation David now found himself in was unfamiliar, and he was unprepared. He was running for his life. Like we so often do, he needed to tell somebody how badly he was being treated by Saul. He first found Samuel the prophet and stayed with him until Saul discovered his whereabouts. He had no food. He was alone. He had no safe place to go. He came to the priest at Nod. Maybe he thought he could find what he needed there—food, counsel, and safety. Instead, his very appearance caused the priest to become fearful. David, himself filled with fear, lied to the priest concerning his visit. He lied to the priest!

Heart under Pressure

What is in the heart will surface under pressure. Potentially troublesome traits often go undetected when things are going smoothly. These traits and behaviors are not necessarily things that are being intentionally concealed. Many times they are things about ourselves that we are unaware of. Yes, we can be unaware of what is hidden inside ourselves. That is a fact that is supported by Scripture: "Because the heart is deceitful and desperately wicked and who can know it" (Jeremiah 17:9). Of course, God knows it, but we remain blinded because the right catalyst to force it to the surface hasn't been applied. Different responses surface as the heat gets higher. That is why it concerns me when I hear individuals say, "I would never do such and such." Certainly, we hope and pray that our response would not be unseemly or diminish the effectiveness of our testimony. However, there are times in our lives we find ourselves thinking, saying, and even doing things we never imagined. The catalyst that caused David's uncharacteristic behavior to surface was fear. Fear causes responses that surprise and throw us into an unexplainable emotional state.

As we grow in the grace of God, we begin to desire to put off everything that might be hidden from others and ourselves. These are not always things that are sinful but could cause us to commit or enter into sin. We are exhorted to put these things off. The writer of Hebrews distinguishes these things apart from sin by saying, "Lay aside the sin and every weight that does so easily beset us" (Hebrews 12:1). Being fully aware that even the hidden things of our hearts are naked and revealed to God, we begin to pray based on the words of Psalm 139:23—24: "Search me, O God, and know my heart: try me and know my thoughts: And see if there is any wicked way in me, and lead me up in the way everlasting." Notice that is something that we pray once we get serious and are really ready to face the fact that we probably have some unpleasant things hidden deep within. We can be set free.

Personally, I add the request to give me courage to accept the help He has already provided for me to put off and abandon what will be revealed once this prayer is prayed. We have the option of doing as James the New Testament writer cautioned—seeing ourselves in the mirror of God's word and choosing to turn away and forget (ignore) what was revealed

(James 1:22—24). However, freedom and the blessings of the Lord are the products of attending to the revealed condition through prayer and obedience to the word of God.

David only asked for and received food and the sword of Goliath, the giant he had killed. Afterward, he left to seek protection elsewhere. His life had now become really complicated and chaotic. The palace was far from being the place to be mentored. We might think this was cruel and that David would not be prepared to reign as king. However, it was just the opposite. It is here that we are reminded again that God's ways of doing things are different from our own. It is also a reminder that God's wisdom is infinite, whereas ours is limited. We must keep in mind that God promises, if we humble ourselves under His mighty hand, we will be exhorted in due time (1 Peter 5:6). It will happen in a manner that all the glory and honor will undeniably belong to the Lord.

Stop Your Crying

This is a fact that God shared with me personally. It occurred in the summer of 2007. I vividly remember the incident. I had been on a women's retreat. There, I saw young women being mentored by a strong well-known spiritual leader. I was so impressed that I expressed my observations to the young women. I told them how privileged I thought they were to be availed of such an opportunity. Personally, I longed to have such in my own life. I felt so underprivileged— at a disadvantage. I felt my spiritual growth was stunted because of the absence of a mentor. I cried then as I had at other times. After returning home, I continued to cry and feel sorry for myself. Suddenly, one day I heard in my spirit, "Stop your crying." Then I heard, "I designed it this way so no one will be able to get any glory out of what I'm doing in your life." Instantly, my tears dried up, and I have not felt that way again. Most importantly, I settled down to stay open to embrace the lessons the Lord continues to send to me in whatever way He sends them.

A Potential Trap

David behaved himself wisely. The importance of this statement includes what David didn't do as much as what he actually did. Yes, he did go out to war as directed. He performed the assigned tasks. What he didn't do was to try to usurp the authority of the king. A number of achievements in his life could have made it so easy for him to fall into that subtle trap. First, he was loved and popular with the people. Second, he had been anointed to become king. Third, he was successful in all his ventures. These are the criteria that have caused many individuals to be coerced into striking out on their own in ministry and other careers as well.

Sadly, many have moved prematurely and suffered shipwreck. They were drawn off the course that God really intended. Afterward, they learned the cruel reality that people will go with you only so far and oftentimes desert you without warning or remorse. Usually, they stay until things don't go their way or they get a better offer. The behavior they demonstrated in the previous location is, more often than not, to be repeated with you. The time often comes that the vow to stand with you is broken. This is a fact regarding human behavior that should be embraced. Jesus lost many of His disciples when His sayings got hard. Then how are we to expect to be treated differently? The humble and God-fearing individual may return with a repentant heart after realizing they had been beguiled. Others will not return mainly because of rebellion and a prideful heart. Oftentimes they cause much damage to ministries and the very impressionable along the way.

Point to Ponder

God's path often leads us in directions we never expected, not to confuse us but to prepare us. When life feels unfamiliar or uncomfortable, remember: His provision is more than enough, His timing is intentional, and every unexpected turn is shaping you for the purpose He ordained.

CHAPTER 9

Asylum in the Enemy's Camp
1 Samuel 21:10 — 15

B eware, God doesn't make an announcement that what we are about to encounter-especially trouble—will work to bring the answer to our prayers. Oftentimes situations begin to develop through which we begin to detect things about ourselves that we had been totally unaware of. The catalyst to cause these things to surface is often tribulations. During these times, things that cast a cloud over God's presence in our lives begin to surface. As they are addressed and removed, the brilliance of the light of Jesus is able to shine through.

I Got It-Can I Keep It?

It would seem that the situation David found himself in was not fair or did not serve any lasting purpose. It is hard to grasp the fact that life is not fair. Additionally, it is not strange that we often cannot see the value or lasting purpose of some of the situations we find ourselves in. Many times they are only revealed in the passing of time.

It gave David the opportunity to exercise the spiritual training he had acquired. It is often said your gifts will get you into a position, but it is your character that will keep you there. It is stated this way in the Bible: "Your gifts will make room for you and bring you before great men" (Proverbs 18:16). Notice it does not mention the gifts keeping you there? Sadly, this fact has been played out before us much too often in the media. Failure to maintain the positions accompanying wealth and fame has been evidenced in the arenas of sports, music, government, and yes, even in the church, Christian community, and school system. This fact has not been isolated to individuals with awesome gifts and a means to escape poverty and the communities wherein they were destined to meet with early death. Their gifts brought them into positions that provided money, fame, open doors, and large followings. A by-product is the responsibility of being a role model to many impressionable young people. Many have failed in this role. The situation has become so prevalent that the question has been raised—why?

Often the attempts to answer that question have come with more questions. Is there no fear of God anymore? What happened to endeavoring to obtain Godly character? Godly character—the ability to do what is right because it is right to do, right? Fear of God—reverencing God to the point of wholeheartedly endeavoring to do the right thing at all times. When the fear of God is ingrained, there is a constant awareness that He sees even what others may not—every creature is naked before God. David trusted God to protect and give him power on the battlefield. Now was he able to trust Him in other matters of his life? It sounds as if he confidently believed that God was concerned about everything that concerned him. It is in the wilderness that certainty of such comes. Therefore, it is not strange that to the wilderness is where David had to turn.

Afterward, with Saul close on his trail, he found himself in the Philistine camp. Now he was in the midst of a rival he had faced many times in battle. What could David have been thinking when he went there? Did he think he would not be recognized? Maybe he was so gripped with fear that he didn't think. Was he traumatized?

Indeed, he was recognized. In fact, one of the servants of the Philistine king questioned, "Isn't this the king, the one they celebrated in song and dance for killing ten thousand?"

Probably feeling trapped and fearing for his life, David, with quick thinking, resorted to playing the role of a madman.He scratched at the gate and let spit run down his beard. The Philistine king said to his servant, "Get him out and away." David's strategy worked perfectly. It got him out of the snare he found himself in.

Point to Ponder

Alone time can be a gift or a prison—it all depends on how we use it. Solitude, when embraced, refines our character, strengthens our relationship with God, and prepares us for the destiny He has planned.

CHAPTER 10

Isolation or Solitude

Being alone is something many people fear. The very idea of being alone, for many, is so devastating that they will accept being degraded, demeaned, and taken advantage of to simply not be physically alone. One problem with that line of thinking is that the presence of a warm body is not a guarantee of not being alone. In fact, many report the existence of having a warm body present but there being no verbal communication, expressions of affection, or physical contact. They have the experience of somebody being physically present, yet they are lonely. The result oftentimes is resentment. The person once thought to take away the sense of loneliness now becomes an object of resentment. The realization of yet being alone and the faulty belief that they must live in such a manner the rest of their lives often also causes depression.

There are two commonly mentioned situations in life that invoke thoughts of being alone. They are isolation and solitude. They are alike but different. They are alike in that they both involve the state of being alone. However, we begin to understand how they differ as we take a look at their intended purpose and resulting outcome.

Isolation

The intent of isolation is identified in the definition "to place by itself," "to insulate." There are many reasons we may experience isolation for short or extended lengths of time. It is something that has both positive and negative ramifications.

Quarantine

The purpose, in some instances, is to restrict individuals from coming into direct contact with others and the outside. The intention in such a situation is for the good of the physical health and safety of the public and oftentimes the patient. It is for the purpose of reducing the possibility of transferring germs, as with the outbreak of a virus or protection for individuals with a weakened immune system.

Power and Control

It is a well-known fact that isolation is a common tactic of an abuser. In this case, the intended purpose is to separate the abuse victim from anyutside contact, including family, friends, and exposure that might provide support and enlightenment. It is accomplished through subtle ways often not detected until much damage to relationships has occurred. Sometimes it is to the extreme of causing the victim to give up their employment under the glamorous pretense of being needed at home for the children and duties of the home. Oftentimes tactics are used to cause the victim to be dismissed from their job. The victim often arrives at a point of giving over their power to the abuser as they lose confidence in their decision-making and even parenting skills. Ultimately, the victim's self-esteem is diminished, personal independence is taken away, and credibility with family and friends is lost. The final intended goal is accomplished—total dependence upon the abuser.

Solitude

Solitude is defined in the dictionary as a state of being alone, a lonely life, a lonely place. The word lonely, in this definition, makes solitude to also be viewed as negative. But is it possible to view solitude as being positive? Is it possible to think of solitude without experiencing the feelings of loneliness, fear, or being needy? Maybe you will experience positive thoughts when solitude is viewed as a special time for introspection, personal growth, personal development, and enjoyment of self.

Solitude, then, may be considered as purposeful aloneness and a personal gift. In fact, a time of solitude is good and needed by everybody. It is during these times that many individuals are personally refreshed and rejuvenated. It is often accompanied by insights to be shared with the public. Things are revealed because the mind is clear and open to hear what the spirit of the Lord will say.

Finally, solitude, unlike isolation, is for the purpose of refining and being enriched. Realization of the benefits that accompany times spent in solitude helps—I repeat, helps—cast off the often accompanying loud controlling woe-is-me phrases, such as "I'm so lonely, so alone," "Nobody cares," or "Nobody loves me."

Not as Intended

I believe isolation is what was intended for David. However, his actions give the impression that he turned it into a time of solitude. There are no indications that David shut down or became immobile or overwhelmed with feelings of being alone, lonely, unloved, and such. Instead, I venture to believe he utilized those times to become intimately acquainted with God. We can see how close of a relationship he cultivated with the Lord in the way he approached dilemmas in his life. In times of sadness, despair, trouble, and uncertainty, he quickly turned to inquire of the Lord for direction.

A solitary place may be where God desires us to retreat to periodically. In such a place, an intimacy with Him can be established, a time and place where we learn to recognize His voice—"My sheep know my voice" (John 10:4A). Such a skill has to be cultivated—it doesn't happen automatically, as many are led to believe. This fact was demonstrated in the life of Samuel, the prophet God used to anoint Saul and David. Samuel learned to distinguish God's voice from others. He had spent time in temple ministry, but he didn't know God's voice. The process by which he came to recognize God's voice is recorded in 1 Samuel 3. The first time God called his name, he went to Eli the priest thinking he had called him. Three times Samuel heard his name being called. Three times he went to Eli thinking he had called him. The third time, Eli told Samuel, "The next time you hear the voice, say, 'Yes, Lord, I'm listening." Samuel did as Eli instructed. That encounter with the Lord marked the beginning of an intimate relationship with the Lord that lasted all the days of his life.

The qualifications presented to King Saul regarding David caused me to ponder, how had David become skilled in the stated areas in his life? David, yet a young person, had spent most of his life in the pastures with sheep, yet he had all these qualifications? When were they developed? I venture to guess they were the result of utilizing his time in solitude. It could have become a time of spiritual and personal enrichment. David entertained difficult to master, yet David was said to be skilled at playing it. He had no armor, shield, or spear when facing the giant Goliath, yet he was victorious through the use of having previously perfected what he had available to him (some sticks and stones). He had been assigned the job of watching and protecting his father's sheep. It was a task that he accomplished through learning to be cunning (artful, using strategy, being crafty) to outwit predators, both animals and bandits, that would come to steal the sheep.

I am certain David's encounters during hard times would have been far different if he had focused on feelings of abandonment, being unwanted, or not liked. Instead, he turned his alone time into productive periods resulting in far—reaching benefits for himself immediately and others during his journey to fulfilling his destiny.

Point to Ponder

Alone time can be a gift or a prison—it all depends on how we use it. Solitude, when embraced, refines our character, strengthens our relationship with God, and prepares us for the destiny He has planned.

CHAPTER 11

Prayer at Mom's House

Times of solitude—I didn't understand them as being positive at first either. By no means do I believe or would attempt to convince anybody that solitude is easy. In fact, it can be difficult—less difficult if the intent of it is understood, but difficult. Solitude is not an easy experience to work through. That fact is understandable because we were created for fellowship. The Bible tells us that God created man for fellowship with Himself. My favorite picture of this relationship comes from the song composed in 1912 by Charles Austin Miles, "In the Garden." It provides a picture of tranquil times of fellowship with the Lord.

Personal Experience

During one of my transition stages, I came to fret over the phone not ringing, no letters or cards in the mail, and such. It was during my times of great insecurity as a born-again Christian. I felt it meant I had no friends, which then translated into the false belief that there had to be something wrong with me. I have since learned that quite often such thinking is a trap, a trap intended to make us to focus on what is nonproductive and a hindrance to our being perfected for our purpose.

I also began to notice that when my time of being alone would become long, God would send someone by phone, mail, TV, or teachings to speak to me. I began to embrace the fact that my time of solitude did not mean that nobody cared about me. Instead, there was a purpose. Actually, I had gotten a glimpse of this in my childhood.

This is a principle I learned early in life. It may sound strange that it was possible for me, being raised the eldest of eleven living siblings and a mother and father in a four-room house. But often, after the noise and continuous activity of the day was over, I'd retreat into my textbooks. It was a solitary place for me to go. The result was the honor of graduating as class valedictorian. This is a practice I've brought forward into adulthood.

As I worked on my doctorate degree, I learned that my temperament is that of melancholy. As such, I need quiet times to reflect and daydream. It is what rejuvenates me. However, whether a melancholy like me or a sanguine, who thrives on having a calendar filled beyond capacity with people to see and places to go, time to still away is necessary. Sue Patton Thoele included in her book *The Courage to Be Yourself*, a number of deposits that should be made in what she calls life accounts to create positive balance which leads to emotional surpluses in life. I found it interesting that one such deposit is solitude.

I finally began to make the connection of my spending quiet time with the Lord and the spiritual victories that were accomplished when I went out. My private worship would be evidenced publicly. They followed the biblical principle of being rewarded openly for prayer and worship done in secret. I have many of such examples, but the one that I'd like to share occurred early in my growth.

Suddenly, one day as I moved about during a time of solitude and quietness, I felt a deep sadness, a feeling of being misunderstood and treated like an outcast. Somehow I knew they were not my own feelings. I was feeling the heart of my mother. She was over eight hundred miles away in Florida. These were feelings we had not discussed. I knew I needed to go to her. The next holiday was Thanksgiving. That would be the time that I would travel to Florida and trust God for the proper time to talk with her.

The Proper Time

The occasion came by way of the call for a prayer gathering to be held in her home. This was a setup by God. You'd have to know my mother to get the full impact of this action. It was such that upon hearing that prayer was going to take place at my mother's, one individual said, out of disbelief and curiosity, "I'll be there."

The hour arrived that individuals were to arrive. I did not know how or when I would have the opportunity to share with my mother what God had revealed to me, so I moved about prayerfully setting up chairs in the living room. Gathered were an elderly brother and sister, the aunt of my friend (the one that admitted coming because of disbelief), and many others. The Lord led me to begin telling the story of my salvation experience. Somewhere along the way, the Holy Spirit took over, and individuals were weeping, clapping, and shouting. Praise God, Mom was on her feet, crying and saying repeatedly, "Nobody knows, nobody knows." There it was! I pulled her into my arms and said, "Mom, God knows, and that is why I am here."

The Lord had given me the awesome privilege of being present when my mother gave her life to the Lord, but that was not all that the Lord did that night. The woman that came out of curiosity was glued to her seat, maybe out of amazement, but I believe out of conviction. You see, she knew the Lord but had walked away from her training. In fact, the only man in the group was her boyfriend. Soon after that meeting, she broke off that relationship, returned to the church, and became faithful until she passed away a number of years later. Many that attended the gathering can still recall that night.

The Lord rewarded me for spending that time in solitude. Because of personally being there, I was able to stand at my mother's funeral years later, looking down at the bodily frame in which she had spent her days here on earth and tell this story. I could tell it feeling assured that, at last, she was with the one that totally understood and had never, not for one moment of her life, cast her aside.

Point to Ponder

Solitude is not empty time—it is fertile ground for God to work, reveal truths, and prepare us to impact others in ways beyond our imagination.

CHAPTER 12

A Place of Refining
1 Samuel 22:1 — 23

Astatement believed to have been made by Abraham Lincoln is "Character is who we are when no one is watching. Good character is doing the right thing because it is right to do the right thing." Expanding further on that thought, we know that good character is not something that we are born with. For ages, it was developed during our formative years through training in the home, school, Sunday school, and involvement in other activities where Godly character was taught and demonstrated. However, for various reasons, this important element of human development has not taken place in recent years. Recognizing their importance, society is attempting to compensate by establishing schools and trainings to instill them in individuals. A number of models are being used. Some overlap in the traits being taught. The most basic include honesty, fairness, loyalty, kindness and caring, respect, integrity, and being a good citizen. Rather than offering a definition for each one, I will refer to them as morality and Godly principles.

These were all character traits needed for success as king. David was God-appointed. Therefore, it was God's responsibility to see that he was prepared for the task—God equips those He calls (Hebrews 13:20 — 21). Isn't that interesting? Many individuals think God calls those who are equipped. However, we see God's searchlight goes out to find one that will trust Him. Trust, along with a willingness and obedience to God's commands, makes for a mighty work to be performed in and through our lives. It is no secret that God is able to perfect even our dormant, overlooked qualities for success in ministry.

David had learned the characteristics of a good shepherd and established an intimate relationship with God (Psalm 23:1). Just like he had been shepherd over his father's sheep—guiding them to green pastures, protecting them from predators, binding up their wounds, chastening them when they continued to stray, carrying them when they were hurt—so would God do for him. These were all skills David had learned while watching the sheep. They would provide the basis for his future success. Watching sheep had provided the qualities of a good leader, but to transition those qualities into actual care of a nation of stubborn and stiff-necked individuals would require further development of those skills. This seasoning only comes through various experiences that seem to arise unexpectedly.

God — Chosen, God — Provided

David's life had been interrupted to bring him to this place and point in his life. He was put in a position where his skills would be further developed. The terms being used today are that of honing, fine-*tuning*, *sharpening, refining*, and/or *perfecting*. He had already been described as a man of war. Several of those characteristics had been demonstrated as he watched over the sheep, but leading a nation of people would be different. He needed to learn the things he would encounter in the position of king. The skills he already possessed needed to be perfected and augmented. It would occur as he cared for individuals that had the ability to rebel, to express their dislike and opposition, who were capable of showing a strong endearing connection and, just as strongly, show anger and turn on him.

David escaped to a cave called Adullam after pretending to be a madman to get out of the camp of the Philistines. It is while there that he probably recorded Psalm 142: "I Cried unto the Lord." It shows he yet trusted the Lord to be his refuge, friend, and helper in the midst of being alone and mistreated. Soon his family heard of his whereabouts and came to him. Uncertain of his own fate, he took them to Moab, the native land of his great-grandmother (Ruth of the book of Ruth), to remain until he would know what God would do for him.

Distressed, indebted, and discontented men also found him. David would become their leader. They would become the catalyst through which he would learn to transition the skills learned out in the sheep pastures to men.

God — Chosen, God — Prepared

God had chosen David. Now He would prepare him for the office for which he had already been chosen and anointed to assume. David would not succeed a family member. He would not carry forward the leadership style and influences of anyone else. God had said, "I have provided me a king." God would be his mentor. He would be specific regarding who could sow into David's life. Certainly, it would not be one that had already failed to obey and carry out His instructions. God would perfect that which He had begun in David's life.

New Environments, New Encounters

New assignments bring new encounters. The new encounters may look the same, but they come with new personalities and new personal, professional, and political agendas. A person will enter the new assignment with good basic skills. Some will even come with experiences obtained doing the same type of job in a different location. Transitioning from one place to another is often believed to be just a matter of changing locations. However, what actually takes place is often not that simple.

David had learned basic skills that would take him far. He had the right foundation. Now those skills were to be tested and perfected in a new environment— in the wilderness. God chose him, so God would provide what was necessary: "I the Lord search the minds and test the hearts of men" (Jeremiah 17:10). It is when under pressure that it is seen whether or not confessions will hold up.

Morality and Godly Principles

Morals and Godly principles instilled in the heart are necessary to govern actions when alone and under pressure. I love the admonition the Israelites received regarding their time in the wilderness: "Remember how the LORD your God led you all the way in the wilderness these forty years, to humble and test you in order to know what was in your heart, whether or not you would keep his commands. He humbled you, causing you to hunger and then feeding you with manna, which neither you nor your ancestors had known, to teach you that man does not live on bread alone but on every word that comes from the mouth of the LORD" (Deuteronomy 8:2——3).

So would it be with David. His time in the wilderness would contribute to preparing him to enter into his destined position. The interruptions he had already experienced in his life and would experience along the way would provide opportunities to shape and test his character.

Point to Ponder

God often places us in refining environments to perfect the character and skills He has already begun developing in us, preparing us for the destiny only He can ordain.

CHAPTER 13

Out of Sight, Not Out of Mind
1 Samuel 22 (Addendum)

S talking, per the National Center for Victims of Crime, is defined as a course of conduct directed at a specific person that would place a reasonable person in fear. The individual called the stalker has multiple resources available to assist in tracking the whereabouts of the targeted victim. Today these includes various types of technology, such as global positioning systems (GPS), computer spyware, or cell phones, just to list a few, because they are increasing constantly. Stalking is so prevalent that the month of January has become stalking-awareness month.

Logically, it would seem the abuser would cease efforts to cause harm once the victim moves out of the abuser's presence. However, that is not always the case. Oftentimes that exacerbates an abuser's rage even more. It is for that reason that victims are encouraged to be especially vigilant during the first three to twelve months after separating themselves from an abusive situation.

David Stalked?

It was hard for David to accept the fact that Saul really wanted to kill him. On multiple occasions, David questioned what he had done to provoke such a response from Saul. We are told David behaved himself wisely. In other words, he did not attempt to avenge himself—instead, he performed whatever duty assigned him by Saul with excellence. When Saul demoted him from being leader of his entire army to only a thousand men, he yet did what was required of him with excellence. That included, time and time again, going out to war against Israel's enemy, the Philistines. The more David behaved himself, the more it was obvious that God was with him. He returned from each war campaign victoriously. Contrariwise, the more David behaved himself wisely, the more Saul responded with anger. What should have pleased Saul only caused him to become angrier. After going far away, Saul continued to search for David.

Never to Go Home Again

Maybe now is the time to address the question that many might be asking: Why didn't David go back home when he realized Saul was trying to kill him? The answer is not explicitly spelled out, but it stands to reason that would not have been a viable route to take. Remember, Saul was the king with power to go and do anything he wanted. He was a man consumed with and driven by jealousy and feelings that everybody was against him. David's family home would not have been a safe place for him or his family.

There could hardly be any place that Saul's power and resources would not extend. It was not sufficient that David was no longer in the palace. Saul still viewed David and anybody that spoke well of him as a threat. It did not matter who that person or people might be. His obsession had driven him to even order the death of eighty-five priests and the inhabitants of the city where they lived.

David was out of Saul's presence. He was no longer winning battles for Israel. Therefore, songs of his exploits were no longer being sung. It should have been enough to give Saul to leave off tracking David. Finally, David had become convinced that Saul wanted to kill him. Therefore, he was running for his life. He could not go back home—he had no home to go back to. He had given up on being able to trust any of his fellow countrymen. Therefore, he began hiding in caves and endeavoring in the wilderness for extended period to stay out of Saul's reach.

Point to Ponder

Even when out of sight, danger or opposition may still pursue us, but wise and faithful conduct coupled with God's guidance provides protection and sustains us through seasons of uncertainty.

CHAPTER 14

The Rescurer Becomes The Victim
1 Samuel 23:1 — 29

The Bible admonishes us in the very first words of Proverbs 4:5 to get wisdom, but it doesn't stop there. It goes on to say, "Get understanding; forget it not." Now the word *understanding*, based on a definition found in the *New Webster's Dictionary* and *Thesaurus*, means "to comprehend," "to recognize as implied although not expressed." There are a number of practices that well-meaning individuals become engaged only to find their intended good deeds result in them being victimized. One such role, especially prevalent in the Christian community, is that of rescuer. It is synonymous to being a caregiver. Rescuers are individuals that automatically forge ahead to the aid and/or defense of another person without consulting with the Lord. Yes, the need may be real. Yes, the desire to help may be noble and in keeping with the tenets of Scripture and that of being a kind person. The question is, is attending to that particular situation God's will for you? Rescuers are generous, self-sacrificing, and easily manipulated. The problem is they often end up being victims.

Some of you are well aware of what I am saying because of having had such experiences. Others are probably puzzled at my statement. Both are probably wondering how this can be. After all, isn't it a spiritual mandate to attend to the needs of anyone we find in need of clothing, food, and shelter? Isn't our love for God questioned if we see a fellow believer in need, have it in our power to lend a hand but turn and walk away?

The answer to both questions is yes. However, herein lies the need for wisdom and understanding. I will enlist the help of Jean M. LaCour, PhD, author of *Counseling the Codependent*: A *Christian Perspective Utilizing Temperament*, to help me help you understand the dynamics at play in such a relationship. This author uses a diagram developed by a respected psychiatrist and teacher by the name of Stephen Karpman. The diagram describes the role of victim, rescuer, and a third position called the persecutor. The diagram is called the drama triangle. It is also called a victim triangle. There are only two main characters but three roles that each of the two players, at some point, could find themselves, likewise is the position either of them assume initially.

The dynamics are such that a needy person signals a need for help (housing, clothing, food, medical care, etc.). Thus far, there is no problem. However, a well-meaning rescuer steps in to lend a hand and a hand and a hand. The victim (needy person) gets stronger through the excessive self-sacrificing efforts of the rescuer but has done nothing to help himself or herself. In fact, they have no intentions of assuming personal responsibilities. Why should they? Eventually, the rescuer picks up on what is happening. The rescuer becomes resentful. The victim realizes it. The rescuer works on mustering up the courage to curtail his/her contributions to the victim's dependence. The victim acts first and turns on the rescuer. Thereby, the rescuer becomes the object of the victim's persecution (being talked about, object of character accusations, destruction of property and more). This is a very simplistic description of this very prevailing dynamic. I said prevailing, and I do mean prevailing in all arenas of life.

Rescue of the Rescuer

David had already demonstrated all the characteristics of a rescuer. He now bordered on falling into that trap again. His actions this time differed in that he had learned to inquire of the Lord before forging ahead. David was on the run from Saul. In the process of seeking safety for himself, news arrived of an impending invasion by the Philistines upon the city of Keilah. Protecting them should have been Saul's responsibility. However, Saul was preoccupied with locating David. Contrariwise, David did not count his life or personal interests above his love for his countrymen. He wanted to run to the city's rescue.

He consulted with God and was told to go. His men, however, did not share his self-sacrificing devotion. They were filled with fear. So once again, David inquired of the Lord. Once again, the Lord told him to go and promised they would be victorious.

Of course, Saul heard of David's current whereabouts. David, likewise, had been told that Saul would come after him there. Would the city feel an allegiance toward David? Evidently, David, as rescuers often do, wanted to think they might. He had probably learned from his experience with Saul not to make such an assumption. Therefore, he made a two-part inquiry of the Lord. First, he asked if Saul was coming to seek for him there. The Lord told him yes. Then he asked the dreaded question, "Will the men of Keilah deliver me and my men into the hand of Saul?" He was given the sad response: "They will deliver you up."

Encouragement after Disappointing News

Certainly, we can imagine the hurt and disappointment David must have felt. Maybe he had not yet really embraced the ramifications of a fear-gripped nation. It was a fear that was imposed on it because of the hatred in their king's heart toward David—their rescuer. But there was one that would not utterly forsake him. It would be Jonathan. Every day Saul searched for David without success. Ironically, Jonathan was able to go directly to David. Doesn't that speak volumes? Saul, with the help of spies posted throughout, could not do what one individual assuredly guided by the Lord could do.

Jonathan came demonstrating the characteristics of a true friend. David, his friend, was afraid and uncertain of what would happen to him. Jonathan risked his own life to get to David. The first thing he said to David was "Fear not." That is the salutation of God's messengers throughout the Bible. The most memorable instances might be those of the angel that came to Zacharias, Mary, and the shepherds in the field. They all came to make an important announcement. Likewise, Jonathan came to speak words that would encourage and strengthen David. He said, "My father will not find you and you will be king." Often we need to be reminded of God's promises. Being assured that God will do what He promised, we are encouraged and strengthened. So it was with David. Jonathan's presence and words provided the encouragement David evidently needed. The rescuer had been rescued. Afterward, they parted company.

My Refuge and Fortress

Samuel had not been able to shelter David; the priest at Nob had not been able to offer him asylum; his enemy, the Philistines, had not as much as kept him as a captive; and the city he had put his life in danger to protect felt no obligation to reciprocate his kindness. Inhabitants of even a nearby city voluntarily informed Saul of his location.

David remained in the location where Jonathan found him. Later, he and his men were on one side of the mountain. Saul and his men were about to compass them from the other side. Just then, Saul was informed of an impending homeland invasion. He needed to make haste to return.

God intervened, and the word spoken by Jonathan—"The hand of my father will not find you" — was fulfilled.

Now he had to be on the move again. Jonathan's visit might have helped him break through the oppressive cloud that hovered over him. Once again, David might have been able to draw on past experiences. He would remember what he had learned while out in the pasture with the sheep. It was there that he had learned he could trust God to protect him. There, the Lord had been his refuge and fortress. There, the Lord had been his shield and buckler. There, the Lord had been his hedge of protection. He would now add the assurance that God would get help and words of encouragement to him even when it appeared to be no way.

Point to Ponder

Even the most selfless acts require God's guidance; a rescuer must discern His will, for without it, noble intentions can lead to vulnerability—but God's provision and faithful friends can turn trials into protection and encouragement.

CHAPTER 15

A Surprising Turns of Events
1 Samuel 24:1—22

There was a time years into my spiritual walk that the Lord dramatically stopped me from making a decision that would have far-reaching consequences. Of course, I had no idea of the depths or implications of such a decision at the time—immediate or long range. I had grown impatient in my pursuit of greater experiences (as I perceived them) with the Lord. I had decided my desire to live a consecrated life was for naught—not necessary. Why couldn't I do what I saw many other professing Christians doing? The Lord had dealt with me previously about watching people. Plain and simple, He had said, "You do what you are supposed to do." Well, here I was again, only this time I had actually made up my mind. I was going to follow the crowd. Why not? I continued to reason within myself.

A Piercing Bright Light

Why not? The answer came that very night. I was sitting in church. Suddenly, our pastor casually walked over to me and said, "Sister Wilder, I want you to sit up front." She then walked away without any further instruction. I was puzzled, but I moved in obedience. I was there in front of the church with no one occupying the chairs next to me. Then suddenly, a light, a bright piercing light, seemed to shine down from the ceiling upon me. I felt as though it was shining right through me. I felt exposed and completely naked. I was certain everybody could see right through me. I was afraid to attempt to move or speak. Actually, I am not sure I could have. At that moment, I knew my life had to be different. I didn't know why, but I was certain I could not live a halfhearted Christian life.

There comes a time in life that a firm decision must be made to place our trust in God and obedience to His word. Many times we think we have, but in fact, we haven't. It becomes difficult to distinguish when we are to take matters in our own hands and when we are to entrust the matter completely—completely and totally—to God. It is not easy for some of us to embrace such a resolute frame of mind. We say we have, but we vacillating back and forth—should I do this, or should I do that? The mere fact that we are vacillating is evidence that we have not totally surrendered the situation to the Lord. The reasons vary. Sometimes we don't believe He's heard us or that we really heard Him. Sometimes we feel He is not moving fast enough. Sometimes we feel we just can't endure another day of life as is. In any case, we often move something that we are convicted of afterward.

I am so happy that I've come to believe that God has a plan for our lives. Jeremiah 29:11 confirms this fact. As such, He is about ordering our steps to fulfill that plan. Many times that requires an interruption in our predetermined and even carefully planned plans. He does it because He knows the immediate and far-reaching consequences of our every action.

Convicted, Confessed

Such was probably the case with David. Saul had come close enough to him that he had cut off a part of his robe. Afterward, he was convicted of his actions. He told his servants, "The Lord forbid that I should do this thing unto my master, the Lord's anointed, to stretch forth mine hand against him, seeing he is the anointed of the Lord" (1 Samuel 24:6). The New Testament lets us know that the Holy Spirit will convict us of sin—that is, He will let us know when we are doing or have done something that is not pleasing to God (John 16:9). David was convicted of what he had done. Rather than attempt to cover it over, he openly confessed his wrongdoing.

You may be saying, "I don't understand. I don't see that David did anything wrong." Therein is the problem. It is the little foxes that destroy the vine. Maybe someone else could have done this thing without being convicted. However, David's destiny was not like any other. Saul was still the person God had placed in office. As such, David had to await God's intervention and promise to avenge him. He had not sinned, but it just wasn't the route God would have him take. His destiny required that he be held to a higher standard.

Leading by Example

There were more far-reaching ramifications. The second thing that came out of this encounter was evidence that he would not lead others into temptation. He would lead by example. Therefore, he needed to also forbid his servants from putting forth their hand against Saul. Think how simple it would have been for him to allow them to do what he could not and excuse it away.

Confronting the Enemy

David never meant Saul any harm. However, he now humbly got Saul's attention and rehearsed the fact that he had the opportunity to kill him. He let him know that he had the opportunity and was also coerced to do it. Then he let Saul know that he had decided to entrust the whole matter to God to judge and avenge.

Complimented by the Enemy

Now Saul was convicted. He said to David, "You are more righteous than I: You have rewarded me good: whereas I have rewarded you evil." He continued to say, "For if a man finds his enemy, will he let him go well away?" (1 Samuel 24:19a) Expressed out of Saul's heart would come strong emotions. He acknowledged that justice and mercy had been shown toward him by David. He also acknowledged his own fault and guilt. However, there was a conflict between the words out of his mouth and his actions. In one breath, he expressed gratitude. In another instance, his expressions were those of uncontrollable anger. His expressions changed based on what was influencing his life at the time—moments of sanity or completely dominated by the evil spirit.

Remain Vigilant

Abuse victims are taught to be alert to the tactics of abusers. The driving force behind their actions is always power and control. One way they attain them is through various types of manipulation. One very common type of manipulation is to apologize for their latest abusive act—physical or emotional. Their words and behavior are to accomplish reconciliation, which is often exactly what the victim has longed to see and hear. The victim's heightened sense of awareness is once again lowered. Sadly, the promises are seldom kept. The abuser returns to being abusive, and the victim is further confused.

Likewise, Saul's seemingly repentant expressions probably encouraged David. However, Saul's history of erratic behavior was cause for David to be discerning. Specifically, Saul said, "I know well that thou shall surely be king and that the kingdom of Israel shall be established in thine hand." That was true, and it sounded as if he were offering David encouragement and support. Caution! Caution! The evil spirit had not been dealt with. It was evident when he proceeded to ask David to swear to him that he would not destroy his seed or his own name out of the kingdom. His efforts to get what he wanted had not been abandoned. It remained as it had been earlier. He wanted his seed (Johnathan) and his name to have prominence.

God is long-suffering toward us throughout our life's journey. The interruptions He allows are never to destroy us. Rather, they are to perfect us. He doesn't always offer explanations. We need to simply trust and obey as He navigates us onto our ordained destination.

Point to Ponder

Trusting God's timing and exercising patience often requires restraint from taking matters into our own hands. True leadership is shown in obedience, mercy, and integrity—even when it means sparing those who oppose us.

CHAPTER 16

The Journey Gets Long
1 Samuel 25:1—44

There hath no temptation taken you but such as is common to man; but God is faithful, who will not suffer you to be tempted above that ye are able; but will with the temptation also make a way to escape, that ye may be able to bear it. (1 Corinthians 10:13)

Most of us have had the experience of traveling a distance with children. Once the trip gets long, we begin to hear from the back seat a continuous chorus of "Are we there yet?" Hearing those words repeated time and time again makes the journey seem even longer. So it is when awaiting the delayed fulfillment of a promise. The delay is often met with discouragement and thoughts of giving up. It is at this point that many find the pressure and struggle of facing life situations—loneliness, financial responsibilities, insecurity, feelings of inadequacy, and such—too difficult. They abandon the course and turn to various self-selected outlets. Many times the answer is near at hand, but the course is abandoned to employ our own ways of getting things done. It is usually right at the brink of a breakthrough. I remember one woman, after having prayed and waited for a husband for a period, saying to me, "God was taking too long, so I did it myself." Needless to say she had much trouble in that marriage.

Our ways may bring temporary relief, but often they prove not to be lasting. Upon realizing the foolishness of such actions, an attempt is made to just return to things as they were. Often more baggage has been collected along the way: another broken relationship, an unplanned pregnancy, or having contracted a life-threatening disease. We carry constant reminders of our ill-fated efforts. These cause frustration because returning to the point of detour is not so simple. Therefore, trying to return to the place you once were is worse. If only we had stayed with the process, God would have come through. God will strengthen us to stay the course if we so desire. The writer of 1 Peter 5:10 offers encouragement with these words: "But the God of all grace who hath called us unto his eternal glory by Christ Jesus, after that ye have suffered a while, make you perfect, establish, strengthen, settle you."

A Temptation Aborted

Such was the case with David. He was on the verge of heading off on a wrong course. He had forfeited his first opportunity to kill Saul. Samuel had died. Now he had moved to another wilderness location. There, he had heard of a rich man whose hired hands he and his men had befriended throughout the time of grazing. Now it was time for shearing. Therefore, it did not seem unreasonable that David would send word by ten of his young men to ask for whatever in the way of food and provisions the rich man would give them. After all, it is likely that if it had not been for their protection, this rich man might not have had anything to shear.

It seems that the rich man and David had never met. Nevertheless, news of the protection his men had provided should have caused some type of bond to be established between them. It seems that David certainly thought so because he gave his men instructions to greet this man in his name. The rich man's reply indicated that such a sense of endearment and bonding wasn't shared. Neither did he feel obligated to express kindness in any manner. Instead, he belittled David's men and sent them away empty-handed.

A Critical Moment

The men returned and reported the incident to David. The report caused David to become extremely angry. His anger probably grew worst as he replayed the incident in his head: *Why did I ever protect that man's property out there in the wilderness while they were near us?* Not a *thing that belonged to him was stolen.* No harm came to his men. This is how he repays me? Continuing to replay the matter in his head, he probably thought he wouldn't have any sheep to shear if he had not shown kindness to his men.

Now fully enraged, he vowed to take matters in his own hands and get revenge speedily. He instructed his men to suit up for war. His plan was to wipe out everybody and everything that belonged to this man by morning. David had deliberately not done anything to avenge himself with regard to Saul. Now was not the time to be tricked into doing something that would cause him anguish later in life. David was probably also weary and tired. A little encouragement would enable him to press on.

God provided this needed encouragement through the rich man's *wife-Abigail*. Upon hearing of the incident, this wise woman made haste to get to David with provisions. She reached David, presented the food, made apologies for her husband, accepted blame for her husband's actions, and convinced David to hear what she had to say. Somehow she recognized that his trouble was a part of preparing him for the throne. She spoke with assurance that he would come through all his trials victoriously. Greater yet, he would come through with clean hands and a pure heart. Specifically, she began to say

• The Lord will make you king and your descendants also because you are fighting His battles. If anyone should try to attack and try to kill you, the Lord God will keep you safe.

• As for your enemies, the Lord will throw them away.

No Regret, No Remorse

A weapon needed for success in life and ministry is that of a good conscience. That is why we must endeavor to do what is right in all matters at all times. The Bible lets us know we have an adversary that is forever accusing those who place their trust in the living God. We are familiar with the story of Job. He was the innocent man that Satan accused of maintaining his integrity only because his physical body had not been afflicted (Job 1:5). Now think about it, how many times have you been hampered from moving forward in areas of ministry because of the sudden remembrance of something wrong or hurtful you said or did far in the past (intentionally or unintentionally)? Why would you remember at that moment? It is because the accuser is at work. His ultimate goal is to block and even stop your progress altogether.

Self—Condemnation

For if our heart condemn us, God is greater than our heart, and knows all things. (1 John 3:20—21)

We have an adversary that is forever at work waging warfare in our mind, but glory to God, we yet have the victory through repentance and the shed blood of Jesus. Through sincere repentance, we are assured that God has forgiven us of our mess-ups. The Bible tells us so in 1 John 1:9, "If we confess our sins, he is faithful and just to forgive us our sins, and to cleanse us from all unrighteousness." That being so, we do not have to entertain the adversary's accusations. We are exhorted to submit ourselves unto God, resist the devil, and He will flee from us (James 4:7). Of course, not being put in such a situation is better. Paul expressed being familiar with such a situation years after David: "Herein do I exercise myself, to have always a conscience void of offence towards God and toward men" (Acts 24:16).

Therefore, it is not strange that Abigail would conclude her plea to David by telling him why the Lord would do all the things she spoke of: "It is all so that when the Lord has done all these things and made you king you will not have to feel regret or remorse for having killed without reason or taken your own revenge." God was shaping David into a man after His own heart. He needed to be able to respond to the question of "Who will enter into the hill of the Lord? Who will be able to stand in His holy place?" (Psalm 24:3——4). The answer follows: "He who has clean hands and a pure heart; who hath not lifted up his soul unto vanity, nor sworn deceitfully." David would have a conscience free of offense in this matter once he became king!

Catastrophe Averted

Upon hearing what Abigail had to say, David pulled back. He recognized that God had intervened keeping him from fulfilling his plans to destroy all that pertained to this rich man. He began praising God for sending Abigail and for keeping him from avenging himself. He took the way of escape, and his rage turned to praise.

Many times we see where others spoke to David of becoming king, but nowhere do we see where David spoke of himself as becoming king. When he took his family to Moab for safety, he asked if they could be left there until he knew what God would do for him. He did not say until God moves Saul and gives him his position. When David was anointed king, there was no great fanfare and public announcement—that would have put Samuel's life in danger. So where were these people getting such information? My guess is that they saw the qualities of greatness in David. Evidently, he carried the traits upon him. Often others see the anointing upon us long before we come to embrace it. Sometimes that is a good thing, and sometimes it is not. In David's case, we can see both good and bad occurring.

The good was that aspirations of being king did not get in the way of his day-to-day endeavors to please God in all that he did. On the other hand, such thoughts as "What more is there but the kingdom for David?" had overtaken Saul.

Point to Ponder

Patience, discernment, and a clear conscience are essential on the journey of life. God often intervenes through others to guide us away from actions that could harm us, shaping our character and preparing us for His purpose.

CHAPTER 17

I Had a Dream
1 Samuel 25 (Addendum)

The prophet Samuel had unexpectedly shown up at David's house some time earlier and had anointed David as directed by God. It had taken place without making the announcement of the purpose. Only God and the prophet Samuel knew that David would become the next king of Israel. Abigail appeared unexpectedly in the fields at the time of shearing with words of exhortation, reassurance, and specifics regarding his destiny. I can only imagine how puzzled yet encouraged David must have been to hear the words spoken by Abigail. God provides the light we need to stay on track to fulfill His plan for our lives.

Strangers Saw It

I am almost embarrassed to say how many times and ways it took for me to finally embrace the office and gifting God placed within me. He had asked me once, "What do you like doing?" I had responded, "Teaching." But I had not embraced it as a gift from God. However, I have much joy in my heart to tell of how longsuffering the Lord was and continues to be with me. Strangers would say, "You're a schoolteacher, right?" My response would shock them. I am an engineer. I am not a teacher. Finally, I got it through a dream.

My Dream

I awakened from a dream about 2:50 a.m. The scene was one in which I was accompanied by two other women in the entryway of a church. A young man and a minister were already in the room. I knew the women but felt it strange because one of the women, though alive in the dream, had actually passed away years prior to the dream. The minister had been doing a series of teachings. He invited us to take a seat. As we sat in the chairs that were there, he moved to another side of the table. Upon sitting, the minister began to talk about how you could really settle into the new chairs, to sit comfortably, versus the old. The young man responded to something the minister was teaching by saying, "That is how I feel." He followed up with a distressing description of what he had thought to do to himself. I first began to ask him some thought-provoking questions. Then I moved around the table and took a seat. The young man continued to expound on what was troubling him. Everybody got quiet as I dialogued with him regarding his situation. I remember being conscious of the minister watching me. I wanted to turn, apologize, and ask for permission to continue. It was then that I awakened.

I prayed for the interpretation. It revealed that there were a number of issues standing in the way of my becoming assured of the calling upon my life. The most liberating were as follows:

Past Influences

Standing Afar Off: That was exactly how I was feeling! I had always felt that other individuals were privileged to have a close relationship with the Lord, a relationship, for some reason, in my thinking, I did not or could ever have. I felt they had spiritual gifts, but I had none.

Apologize and Ask Permission: I grew up always feeling the need to complete a great many tasks to earn permission from my earthly father to engage in activities-religious, educational, and recreational. I had carried that from childhood over into adulthood. Therefore, I had not been able to acknowledge the thing that was so obvious to others. I awaited permission.

Suddenly Awakened: It was significant that I awakened at that moment. In the dream, I was embracing my gift of teaching. The dream was interrupted because I didn't need to seek permission to flow in the God-appointed gifting. I need only to operate by and through the Holy Spirit. Then and there, I prayed that I be delivered from this hang-up and its cause be rooted out.

Freed to Move Forward

The Chairs: As we sat in those chairs, the minister began to talk about being able to really settle into the new chairs. He talked of sitting comfortably in the new chairs as opposed to the old chairs. That was what I needed to do with the gifting from God. Rest in it, settle into it, exercise it. Thereby, I would gain much confidence.

The End: Joy and thanksgiving were my expressions. What a dream-deliverance and healing! I began to praise and thank God. He had interrupted my night season to reveal areas of insecurities and uncertainties in my life. They were hampering me from coming into agreement with God's report regarding my life. The interpretation of that dream had done for me what I believe Abigail's visit had done for David.

An Ancient Asiatic Custom
Fleeing from the Dart

When a dart was thrown at a freed-man, and he escaped from it by flight, he was thereby absolved from all allegiance to his master. Thus Saul by his murderous fury gave complete liberty to David, whose subsequent acts of war against the king could not be considered rebellion. David was no longer a subject of King Saul.

—Handbook of Bible Manners and Customs, p. 139

Point to Ponder

God often uses unexpected moments—dreams, strangers, and quiet revelations—to confirm His calling in our lives. When we finally embrace what He has already placed within us, we step into the freedom and purpose He intended all along.

CHAPTER 18

Déjà Vu
1 Samuel 26:1—25

T he term déjà vu is defined by Wikipedia, the free encyclopedia, as a French term that means "already seen." It is said to be a strong sensation that an event or experience currently being experienced has been experienced in the past, regardless of whether it has actually happened. In life, we often have such situations arise again and again. We suddenly find ourselves in a place or doing something that seems like a repeat from a prior time. I have come to believe these situations resurface either because I didn't pass the test the first time or to confirm I embraced the lesson of the first incident.

This latter scenario is precisely the reason I believe this next event occurred at this point in David's journey—that is, he would be faced with a situation that had all the resemblance of an earlier experience. David's countrymen knew he was hiding in the nearby hillside. Like before, they betrayed him. Again, they went to Saul to inform him of David's current whereabouts. Like before, Saul came searching for David. This time he came with an army of men five times the size of David's small band of six hundred. David was also informed of Saul's location. Saul was headed in the wrong direction. The logical thing for David would be to stay where he was or, at the very least, move on in the opposite direction.

Sadly, David had not accepted the fact that he had done nothing to cause Saul to turn on him. He yet wanted to know the reason Saul desired to take his life. Therefore, he didn't do what was logical. Instead, like before, he entered Saul's camp while he and his men slept. His nephew Abishai (his sister Zeruiah's son) accompanied him.

The time of running from Saul had been long. David had the opportunity to take Saul's life previously but had vowed to trust God to fight his battle. Now he was given a similar opportunity. Once again, he was coerced to kill Saul. His nephew even offered to swiftly perform the task for him. Then his need to spend his days in the wilderness and hiding in caves would be over. After all, he had done nothing to provoke such treatment. Furthermore, the ancient Asiatic custom called fleeing from the dart qualified him to be relieved of any act of rebellion. That was true if he had not decided that his actions would be governed by a higher authority—the Lord rather than the customs of the land. Accepting the offer of his nephew would not render him guiltless in the matter. The law of the land today would consider him a co-conspirator. Certainly, God would see the matter in much the same way.

A Matter of Integrity

David's response might be what set him apart from others and put him in a place to be elevated by God. He was being governed by a law and custom higher than that of man. The time of running had been long, and Saul had escalated his efforts to locate and kill David. But those would not be reasons for David to take matters in his hands. He responded to his servant's request by saying, "Who can lay a hand on God's anointed and be guiltless?" In similar words as before, he said, "As surely as the Lord lives, He Himself will strike him; either his time will come and he will die; or he will go into battle and perish. But God forbid that I should lay a hand on God's anointed" (1 Samuel 26:9——11).

I think those words were not for his nephew's sake alone. I believe they also reflected the fact that he had embraced the lesson of his first encounter with Saul. So rather than laying a hand on Saul, he took things that belonged to him. He took Saul's spear and cruise of water to prove he had been there. Once again, as before, he stood afar off and called over to Saul's camp. This time he addressed Saul's armor bearer, Abner. David had been Saul's armor bearer for a short while. David first commended Abner for being a valiant warrior. Again, we see that David yet had great concern for Saul in that he scolded Abner for not diligently performing his assigned task of protecting Saul. He had taken things that belonged to Saul for the purpose of demonstrating this fact.

Still Searching for an Answer

David's actions were not unlike many during times of unexplained upheavals in life. We struggle to understand the reason for the breach in a relationship. We question and sometimes even plead with the other person to explain what happened. If that approach fails, we begin to assume the blame. We question what we might have done to cause the problem. *What did I do? What didn't I do?*

That too often leaves us without answers or understanding. So it seems it was with David. He had inquired of both Saul and Jonathan as what he might have done to cause the breach in their relationship. In a manner similar to this incident, he had again pressed Saul for understanding. Saul had not, and strange as it may seem, he probably could not give him that understanding.

A Moment of Personal Reflection

David must have dreamed while in the fields. Dreams concerning one's destiny are usually of something great. Certainly, the position David now found himself in would not have been part of his dream. Based on your personal experiences, you can probably imagine David at some point sitting and trying to reason, *Why? I wonder why?* So much trouble for something I didn't seek after. I was out doing my own thing-keeping my father's sheep. So *why is King Saul treating me so badly?* I've only done him good. I behaved myself wisely. I was only performing the task for which I had been assigned. I was concerned for the army of the living God when I slaughtered the Philistines. Certainly, I never asked the women to name me in their songs of praise.

I Wonder, I Wish

I wonder if David ever sat and pondered, Why am I left with this responsibility? I am now responsible for men that I did not campaign or seek out. I now have individuals looking to me for their very survival.

I wonder if he ever asked, "Why me?" saying, "I was perfectly content out there in the pasture with the sheep." There, he was in a familiar place, not the best but familiar. He knew where danger lurked. He knew the trails and what to expect out there.

I wonder if he replayed in his mind all the kindnesses and acts of obedience he had performed in fighting the Lord's battles and helping others. I wonder how many times he asked, "What could I have done differently?

Now he was probably saying within himself, *I wish Samuel the prophet had not come to my father's house that day. I wish I had never been summoned to come to play music when Saul was in trouble. I wish my father had never sent me to the battlefield to check on my brothers. I wish I had never offered to fight Goliath even if he was presenting a threat to my people—Israel. Now I am out here with no home, no familiar place of my own to lay my head. Trouble, trouble on every side!*

From General to Specific

There had to be an explanation. What was standing in the way of true reconciliation? This time, David confronted Saul with specific possibilities. He pleaded with Saul, saying, "If the Lord has stirred you to do this, then let Him accept an offering. But if the problem is due to the false report of men, causing me to be driven out of my homeland, then a curse be upon them." He yet had not conceived of the possibility that the reason Saul wanted to kill him had nothing to do with anything or anybody other than Saul himself.

Another Emotional Plea

As in previous times, Saul offered no explanation for his behavior toward David. He was, however, convicted of wrongdoing. He admitted knowing that his life was precious to David. He acknowledged he had played the fool and erred exceedingly. He offered an emotional plea asking David to return. He promised David to never attempt to do him harm again.

So Familiar

Can you imagine David thinking, Haven't I been here before? *Haven't I heard those words before? What is different with Saul's plea now? Did he say he was sorry? If so, were the words spoken from a place of true remorse or was it that my behavior shamed him? Was he truly remorseful?* David was left having to decide to believe Saul's plea was genuine as his heart had long desired or simply another manipulative attempt to get him to return once again.

Point to Ponder

Sometimes God allows familiar trials to return—not to torment us, but to reveal how much we've grown. Déjà vu moments remind us that integrity is measured not by what we feel, but by what we choose to do. When we let God fight our battles, we pass the test not by winning, but by trusting.

CHAPTER 19

I Will Perish If I Stay
1 Samuel 27:1—4

Reconciliation is the act of making friendly again says the *Merriam-Webster* Dictionary. It is a renewal of friendship. Inherent in the definition is a picture of a prior absence of peace and distance between at least two individuals. Therefore, reconciliation can only occur if it is the sincere desire of v parties. There is no greater example of this fact than that of the scripture: "God in Jesus reconciling us to himself" (2 Corinthians 18). God, by way of giving His Son, has extended an olive branch (offer of peace), but His offer has to be accepted

Therefore, it is obvious that reconciliation is a desire of God's heart. Therefore, we should not think it strange that it is also present in the heart of anyone characterized as a man after God's heart. Indeed, David had desired to be reconciled to Saul. Twice prior to this incident, he had believed Saul was sincere in desiring reconciliation. The fact of the matter was that Saul had not upheld his vow to leave off attempting to kill him on either of the two prior occasions. Saul's pursuit of David had continued..

James M. Freeman, author *of Handbook of Bible Manners and Customs*, stated that David had within his rights to rebel against King Saul. Saul had repeatedly attempted to kill David. He was forced to escape for his life. Like the partridge, an innocent bird that flies away without resisting the efforts of an attacker, David had chosen to finally remove himself from Saul's life-threatening attacks. He never rebelled and never sought revenge. Instead, he continued efforts to identify the issues that were causing the break in their relationship. David wanted to know the cause for Saul's fierce anger and relentless pursuit. However, this time David realized more was needed for reconciliation than Saul's acknowledgment of wrong. He could not trust that it was sincere. It would have to be to bring about the desired change. It could not occur simply because David desired it.

An Often-Asked Question

It became tiring as I began to outline the details of the many times Saul attempted to kill David. In fact, it was so exhausting that I could not complete that line of study in one setting. While doing the study, I kept thinking, *Why did David stay there so long? Why did he keep putting himself in harm's way?* As I awakened the next morning, the answer came to me: David's behavior was consistent with the traits exhibited by individuals living in abusive situations. I was asking the same questions about David as people *often ask* of domestic violence victims: "Why didn't they just leave?" The answer is multifaceted and extremely complex for the astounding number of individuals that are experiencing this hidden-but in-our-faces epidemic. The information given us about David might give some clues regarding his reasons.

Life at Home

We are not given any indication of David complaining about his life at home. However, we could easily reason that he desired more for his life. There was the incident at the feast when he would have been totally left out if Samuel the prophet had not inquired of his father, "Are there any more?" This was after all of David's elder brothers had come before Samuel as he sought the one that God had sent him there to anoint. David had not been called to the sacrifice. Now he would be summoned because of Samuel's inquiry. I tend to think this was not an isolated incident. Then we see how his brother greeted him when he arrived at the battle site with provisions from their father: "Why have you come down here? And with whom have you left those few sheep?" (1 Samuel 17:28b) It seems his contribution to the family was minimized.

Life Away from Home

There was a tremendous contrast in the treatment he received in the palace. David was immediately liked by Saul. King Saul valued and rewarded his talents by placing him in charge of the armed men. He was so pleased with him after killing Goliath the Philistine that he took him that very same day into his home. Jonathan, Saul's son, loved David so much that he stripped himself of his royal garments and gave them to David. That act was the customary way of showing a person respect, confidence, and affection. Additionally, he and David entered into a covenant together.

These were experiences probably unlike any he had with his own family. Saul was the man that had acknowledged and respected his skills. In the palace, David had received recognition and inclusion and was celebrated for his skills. It's not a stretch to see how an emotional attachment could have been formed between David and Saul. Such an attachment would cause David to have trouble accepting the fact that Saul intentionally desired to kill him. Can you imagine the anguish that David might have been experiencing? "This was the man that said he loved me. How could he want to kill me?"

It Must Be My Fault

I can envision David pondering his own actions and retracing his own steps over and over and over again. Each time he must have arrived at the same point of confusion and disbelief. *But I behaved myself as I should in all things. What did I do to cause Saul's behavior? I must have done something. It must have been my fault.* The reality that he had no control over Saul's behavior was hard for David to embrace.

It is painful when forced to see the flaws in someone with whom we have become intimately acquainted. The flaws were probably always there. However, oftentimes the trappings of an abundance of things and activities (travel, social status, money, and such) entice an individual to overlook and make excuses for obvious damaging flaws. Many times it is only when the bad gets to the point of outweighing the benefits that the reality of the situation can no longer be masked. It is then that the situation must be acknowledged for what it is.

Moment of Acceptance

On multiple occasions, David tried to appease Saul. Finally, after fifteen attempts on his life, David accepted the fact that Saul truly intended to kill him. Anyone who has stayed the course and successfully transitioned into a totally unforeseen place in life can usually look back and remember the moment they decided they had negotiated enough; questioned themselves enough; cried enough; and wished, prayed, and waited for someone to rescue them long enough. The moment of "enough is enough" arrives. It is like awakening out of a deep sleep and being able to see the situation for what it is. Needless to say, we ask ourselves, "Where have I been? Why was I not able to see this before?" It is often at that moment that the decision is made to close the door on the past. The decision is made to let go of the thing(s) or person(s) so much time had been spent trying to hold on to.

There comes a point in situations such as David's that there is no turning back. It is a time and place in the process where you have learned enough about the dysfunction of your past to understand that even if enticed to turn back again, things would never be the same or would never be as you so desperately hoped they would be. It is a place that is totally unfamiliar.

Fortunately, it is then that something comes from deep within ourselves giving a never-before-realized strength and resolve to arise and go forth. Fear and excitement simultaneously provide the needed strength and determination to live and not die. The fear that once caused immobility suddenly offers the energizing fuel needed to go forward.

Facing Reality

That is where I believe David had arrived. It seems he finally grasped the reality of the situation. All his efforts to broker a peaceful relationship between him and Saul had been fruitless. Restoration would require both parties to put forth sincere efforts to identify and settle the troublesome issues. David had come to realize what he was trying to achieve was not what Saul desired. Therefore, all his appeals, reasoning, and showing of kindnesses would not be sufficient to change Saul's heart toward him. Saul's one and only desire with regard to David was for him to be dead.

David could now admit "I will perish if I stay here." He still did not know the reason for his life being in danger, but he believed Saul would succeed in killitng him if he remained within his sphere of influence. Where could he possibly find a place of refuge? Was there a place that the one who sought him as a partridge was too afraid to approach? Was there a place that the residents would not fall prey to King Saul's intimidation and manipulation ploys to reveal his location?

Indeed, there was such a place. It was in Philistine territory. There had been war against Israel and the Philistines all the days of Saul's reign. Saul would not search for him there. Therefore, David reasoned within himself that he should speedily escape into the land of the Philistines. Strange as it seems, David, the killer of Goliath, the Philistine's giant, believed he would find refuge with them.

Point to Ponder

There comes a moment when God opens our eyes to a truth we can no longer ignore. Like David, we must sometimes step away from what is familiar—no matter how deeply we long for reconciliation—and choose the path that leads to life. Courage begins when we finally say, "I will perish if I stay," and trust God enough to walk toward the unknown He is calling us to.

CHAPTER 20

The Enemy Wants Your Mind
1 Samuel 27:5—12

We often hear the saying "What a difference a day makes." That is an expression used in response to a sudden and drastic change in a situation. It is also used to remind ourselves of the fact that a seemingly unchangeable situation can change. The emphasis is that timing is of the utmost importance. An action taken too soon or too late can result in negative consequences.

David and his men had been on the run from Saul and engaged in various battles long enough to make the Philistine king believe he was now alienated from Israel. This made it possible for David to now seek asylum in Philistine territory. David had appeared in the Philistine camp previously. The first time, he was frightened and alone. This time he came as an acclaimed warrior with a small band of fighting men. This time he found favor with the Philistine king. This time he asked for a city where he and his men could dwell. This time the king granted his request. He was given a city called Ziklag.

What's in It for Me?

What had changed from David's first visit? I dare believe the difference boiled down to whether or not David had anything to offer the king. During his first visit, it appeared that his mind was gone. There was nothing that could be captured, taken away, controlled, or manipulated. Therefore, what could he offer the king? This time David returned with full evidence of being clothed in his right mind. His abilities as a leader and warrior were evident. Furthermore, the Philistine king believed they had a common enemy the Israelites. "Therefore, he shall be my servant forever," said the Philistine king. He had big plans for David. They included having David accompany them into battle against Israel. Interestingly, the Philistine king recognized David's skills as an asset. Ironically, they were the same skills that Saul viewed as a threat.

The Mind

The response of this king vividly demonstrates the reason for the battle in which we must continually engage. That is the battle for our minds. It is the mind that always comes under attack. That is because it is only by getting control of our minds (thoughts) that the enemy is able to exercise control over our lives. His aim is the mind so he can accomplish his purpose to kill, steal, and destroy (John 10:10a). His tactic is to draw us into sin. James 1:15 informs us of the fact that once sin is completed, spiritual death and oftentimes physical death follows. A dead thing is of no use to anyone. It is to be put out of sight. The Philistine king Ashish vividly expressed that fact during David's initial visit.

Another Observation

A fact I find equally important to mention is that, first, David, although rejected during his earlier visit, had the courage to first return to the Philistine camp. Second, he had the courage to ask for what he wanted. He was not paralyzed by the fear of rejection. Instead, he demonstrated that he wasn't carrying around baggage with which individuals with his background are often plagued. He was demonstrating the characteristics of a man after God's heart-bold, courageous, direct, and intentional. I dare believe these characteristics could only begin to surface after he released himself from exerting efforts to reconcile with Saul. This is a point that might have been hidden, as it is often concealed from individuals in unhealthy relationships. Sometimes there are characteristics that friends and family members once observed, sometimes they are such that recently acquired acquaintances find amazing. Unlike family and close friends, they had not been privileged to observe such strengths.

An Unfaltering Allegiance

During David and his men's stay in Philistine territory, raids were conducted against other enemies of the Israelites. He would respond to the Philistine king's inquiry regarding the location of his raids by simply saying against the southern area of Judah or against the southern area of the Jerahmeelites

69

or against the southern area of the Kenites. The named cities were Israelite cities. David, indeed, raided the areas south of these cities. However, the occupants of these southern cities were enemies of the Israelites. What Ashish heard was that David had raided Israelite cities. Thus, he was convinced that David was an outcast to the Israelites. However, David was still fighting the Lord's battles. His allegiance was still to Israel. He further demonstrated it by sharing the bounty taken during their raids with the nearby Israelites.

Many debate whether David was deceptive in his response to Ashish. Many also think David failed to trust God's continued protection by going into Philistine territory. The fact of the matter is David had experienced wenty-one attempts on his life, three attempted reconciliations, and betrayal by those he risked his life to help. Somehow I personally see his way of escape from the grasp of Saul as daring, risky, and requiring a greater trust in God's protection than ever. But time would tell.

First, I bring your attention back to the fact that we need not let the enemy know our every planned move. I do not feel that David lied. He had raided cities south of Judah. I believe God caused Ashish to hear what he wanted to hear.

Second, I can only say awesome, awesome. David asked Ashish for a city, but he didn't say what city. He didn't say where it was to be. Isn't it ironic that he was given a city that bordered Judah? In fact, it was a city that had been apportioned to Simeon (Joshua 15:5). However, it evidently had been taken by the Philistines in one of their battles-a city away from Saul, far away from Ashish, and yet nearby the people David so loved and desired to protect. How strategic!

Finally, concerning the view of many that frowned on David's decision, some feel that he no longer trusted God. Personally, I find it "so God" that David had voiced concern during his last meeting with Saul that his probable accusers were sending him away from his inheritance to worship other gods. But David had, all along, respected his God-Jehovah. It is a fact that God sometimes uses our enemies to position us for blessings. That is the way I see the hand of God in this situation in both David coming into Philistine territory and being given the city of Ziklag. He was far away from the enemy of his own country and far away from the enemy in whose territory he now resided that he could worship as he pleased. The location of Ziklag worked perfectly for David. It was located two days' journey away from the Philistine camp. He was out of Saul's reach. Additionally, he was able to continue to fight the Lord's battles. He and his men could continue to engage in raids against Israel's enemies without their exploits being detected by the Philistines. Shrewd, shrewd—don't you think?

Point to Ponder

The enemy knows that if he can capture our minds, he can influence our steps. But like David, we are called to guard our thoughts and remain anchored in God's truth—no matter where life takes us. Even in unfamiliar territory, God can turn what was meant to destroy us into a strategic place of protection, purpose, and victory. Keep your mind stayed on Him, and watch how He works all things together for your good.

CHAPTER 21

Don't Let the Devil Ride
1 Samuel 28:1—25

Throughout our life's journey, we will be faced with troublesome situations. Some will come upon us unaware and affect us deeply. The depths in which we are affected are usually governed by what is lodged in our hearts and memories of past experiences and such. There could be a whole myriad of conditions lying dormant within. Some of which we often do not realize at the time. That is another reason I believe God so often causes an interruption in our lives. Hindsight often makes us look back and realize that situations we thought were for our demise were nothing of the kind. Afterward, we see they were catalysts to bring a potential troublesome situation to the surface. Now whether we humble ourselves and deal with the problem or not is another matter.

It will always behoove us to not sweep matters that have been exposed under the rug, thinking they will go away. The soloist Neal Roberson sings a song titled "Don't Let the Devil Ride." The simple lyrics are "Don't let the devil ride." He goes on to tell the consequences of ignoring this plea. "If you let him ride, he'll want to drive. Then if you let him drive, he'll take you too far." The artist's plea is simply don't let him ride. Sin and the devil are synonymous. Jesus told us in John 10:10 that the goal of the devil is to kill, steal, and destroy. He accomplishes his goal through drawing us into sin. Therefore, we should take the words of this song to heart-sin will take you too far. My guess is the artist was voicing Paul's warning to the Ephesians: "Give no opportunity to the devil" (Ephesians 4:18b). Saul, by not attending to the condition of his heart, had, in essence, allowed the enemy to ride. Now we see him being driven even further into the clutches of the enemy.

Result of Wrong Counsel

The signs of Saul having emotional problems were present early. Sadly, rather than properly addressing the issues, he accepted the counsel of individuals that encouraged him to seek help to soothe the evil spirit when it raged. They probably meant well. However, they could not give something they did not have. Fault, therefore, must be placed in its proper place. We are told that in the multitude of counselors, there is safety (Proverbs 11:14). Additionally, we are instructed to not walk in the counsel of the ungodly (Psalm 1). Plain and simple, seeking out counsel is okay. However, knowing the source from which the counselor gets his/her counsel is of utmost importance. The fact is that Saul had access to Godly counsel. Sadly, they were individuals he had not respected nor taken their earlier counsel to heart.

Temporary Relief for a Recurring Problem

Soothing would only provide temporary relief. The problem would resurface again and again. Sadly, it would happen at unexpected times without warning. Soothing would allow it to grow worse. Saul needed to come clean before God in true repentance and receive deliverance. The full ramifications of neglecting to attend to his problem properly were about to take him to the place of no return.

The Philistine army gathered for battle. Saul now found himself facing an impending battle with the Philistines with no word from God. Additionally, his warring men began to scatter. His heart was overwhelmed with fear. He could only think of one solution: He would do the very thing that had been forbidden. He would engage the service of a woman with a familiar spirit (a medium) to bring up Samuel. Such activity was condemned. In fact, Saul himself had enacted this law in obedience to God's command. He would be driven by fear to do what he knew was wrong.

Bowing to a Dead Thing

We are told that when Saul perceived that Samuel had been contacted from the dead, he stooped with his face to the ground and bowed himself. These are acts that signify humility—admitting the need for help. Sadly, yet prevalent today, advice is being sought from the dead rather than the living. It shows how far away from right standards the sin of Saul's heart gone unchecked had caused him to drift. Words found in the book *Strength to Love* by Martin Luther King Jr. summarizes what was happening to Saul: "Evil has a self-defeating quality." How true! How sad we also often fail to avail ourselves of the opportunities to address these issues when life's interruptions occur. If only Saul had bowed before Almighty God to ask for forgiveness, he would have received deliverance (cleansing) and healing ("If we confess our sins God is faithful and just to forgive and cleanse from all unrighteousness," 1 John 1:9).

Point to Ponder

The enemy only needs a small invitation to take us farther than we ever meant to go. Saul's life reminds us that unchecked wounds, wrong counsel, and quick fixes can slowly pull us away from God's voice. But every interruption in life is a chance to turn back before the damage deepens. When we bow to God instead of our fears, He not only forgives— He restores, guides, and keeps us from letting the devil ride.

CHAPTER 22

Way of Escape Provided
1 Samuel 29:1—11

I believe every reader can remember getting into a situation that seemed to be the best available option at the time. However, as time passed, you found yourself in another situation because of your prior decision that seemed not to have a good way out. At such a time, a way of escape can only come from the Lord. Thankfully, that is not out of the realm of possibility. In fact, we are left with such a promise: "God will not let us be tried beyond our strength. He will give us the strength to bear it or a way of escape" (1 Corinthians 10:13b).

David and his men had enjoyed the favor of King Ashish and freedom from the pursuit of Saul for a year and half. King Ashish trusted David and believed that he no longer held any allegiance to Israel. This trust was apparent as David and his men—by request of King Ashish—gathered with the Philistines for battle against Israel. The march began with them bringing up the rear of the Philistine army alongside the king.

However, the Philistine princes were less trusting than their king. They had not forgotten David's great exploits and victories against them on prior occasions. They feared he would use this occasion to turn on them in the midst of battle to regain favor with Saul. They were not willing to chance it, so they insisted that David return to Ziklag. King Ashish was given the task of ordering David and his men to depart and return to the city that had been given them.

A Heavenly Intervention

Can you imagine what might have been going through David's mind as the march toward the battleground began? Can you imagine the relief he must have felt upon being told to return to Ziklag? I imagine he had to pretend to be disappointed. He reverted to asking the question he had asked on a number of occasions previously: "What have I done?"

Months earlier, he had posed that same question to Jonathan with regard to Saul's treatment toward him: "What have I done? What is my iniquity? What is my sin?" Later, having the opportunity to confront Saul himself, he asked, "Why pursue me for what have I done?" or "What guilt is in my hand?"

Possibility One—A Flashback

Was he momentarily taken back to similar situations in his life, like the time he came to the battlefront to check on his brothers? His brother had expressed his job of watching the sheep as insignificant: "Where have you left those few sheep?"

Possibility Two—Fear

On prior occasions, the question was because of honest confusion. This time it might have carried a different motive. Maybe it was simply to glean a response of discovery. Had his campaigns against enemies of his fellow Israelites been discovered?

Possibility Three—Disappointment

There is a third possibility. Was it possible he really wanted to engage in this war against Israel? Personally, I believe that was a remote possibility. Nevertheless, it is possible that his response was one of true disappointment. Perhaps it would have been as the Philistine commanders feared. Perhaps it would have been for what seems really unlikely to show further loyalty to the Philistine king. Is that what he meant when he told King Ashish, "Surely thou shalt know what thy servant can do" (1 Samuel 28:2)?

In either event, it would not have been conducive to the fulfillment of God's plan for his life. Contrary to the way things appeared, God was yet working on his behalf. God had David's future in mind. God's intervention, as had been Abigail's actions, was to ensure David an expected end.

Many times we draw strength and encouragement from the scripture that tells us that all things work together for good to them that love God and are called according to His purpose (Romans 8:28). Certainly, we have no doubt that David loved the Lord. Equally, we have no doubt that he was called and chosen by God. His life had not been interrupted to cause him needless anguish. His purpose and destiny was to become king of the united kingdom of Israel. God was still bringing good out of every situation David found himself in. They were all working to position and qualify him for the task ahead.

Point to Ponder

Even when our choices place us in difficult corners, God's mercy can still create a door of escape. David's release from the battlefield was no coincidence—it was divine intervention. When we trust God with our missteps as well as our victories, He turns every path, even the confusing ones, into steps toward His purpose. God always provides a way out, not to shame us, but to lead us back into alignment with His will.

CHAPTER 23

Response under Pressure
1 Samuel 30:1—20

O ften we say things like "I would never tolerate such and such" or "I would never do or take that" or even "I will not be like that." Each statement implies we know beforehand how we would respond if faced with similar situations. Such statements further imply we are able to always be in control of our emotions. The truth of the matter is that our actions and responses to situations come from what is in our hearts. Therefore, if we have never personally encountered the specific situation and area of life, we can only hope to behave properly.

Personally, I have learned to refrain from voicing such strong statements. Instead, you might hear me say something like "I pray I would not do such and such." The reason is "The heart is deceitful above all things, and desperately wicked: who can know it" (Jeremiah 17:9). Often the way we think we would respond versus what we actually do when faced with certain situations turns out to be far different. An example would be when Peter, a disciple of Jesus Christ, empathically declaring his allegiance to Jesus, said, "If everyone else deserts you, I won't." He went even further to say, "I will die first" in response to Jesus saying that he would indeed deny Him, not once but three times that very night. Mentally, Peter probably believed that he would never do such a thing. I am sure Peter meant well. After all, he had not actually faced such a situation. How could he know that fear for his own life would override the emotional words uttered out of his mouth?

God, from time to time, allows situations to come our way to expose the condition of our hearts. Take note God does not tempt us. However, He does test us. He does it because "The trying of our faith is more precious to Him than gold that has been tried in the fire" (1 Peter 5:7). It is important to God that we are able to remain standing during the storms of life. It is our confidence and blessed assurance of God's ability to carry us through trying situations whatever they may be—that helps steady us in times of trouble. On one occasion, Jesus pondered, "Will I find faith when I return" (Luke 18:8). It is through life experiences that we both discover what is in our hearts and gain knowledge and wisdom from which to draw in life. Oftentimes these faith—testing experiences come by way of tribulations or troublesome situations.

A common cliché is that trials come to make us strong. The fact of the matter is that trials reveal what is really in our hearts. I find it interesting that God told the Hebrews as they came out of bondage to the Egyptians and journeyed toward their promised land that He led them into the wilderness to humble, to prove, and to know what was in their hearts and whether they would keep His commandments (Deuteronomy 8:2).

Unfortunately, trouble often comes as a thief in the night. In other words, it comes without warning, unexpected, without time to brace ourselves. That causes a reeling and rocking—a shaking of the very foundation(s) that we thought was solid and unshakeable. We experience it in our marriages, in our finances, on our jobs, and even in our assigned ministries. It is often after the fact that we see the handiwork and wisdom of God in our situations. While we were knocking, kicking, and trying to change things or sometimes even trying to keep things from changing, we are really hindering God's efforts to protect us. Sometimes His efforts are to usher us into something better.

Shaky or Solid Foundation

Upon arriving back at Ziklag, David and his band of men found that the Amalekites had taken revenge by raiding their camp and taking their families. When they were told to return to Ziklag, how could they have known their own family needed them? God knew!

Initially, David and his band of men wept aloud together until they had no more strength to weep. Then the same men that had enjoyed many victories and taken much spoils along the way, been protected and taught what it was to show respect and be respected, now turned on the one individual that had received them unto himself.

It didn't matter to these men that David's family had also been taken. The only thing that mattered to them was their families were gone. They needed a place to direct their anger and pain. They needed to blame somebody, so they turned and spoke of stoning David. Now what would David do with all his emotions, the hurt and concern he felt for his family, the distress caused by those that turned on him?

An Option

A leader must face the possibility of being abandoned by even the one(s) given most attention. God graciously reminded me during another of my times of testing that they did it to Jesus. Isn't that a sobering thought? If Jesus's followers deserted him when things got hard, do we dare expect to be treated differently?

I have had a number of woe—is—me occasions in my spiritual journey. I have often wanted to distance myself from everyone and everything that I felt was contributing to my anxiety and sadness. During one such occasion, the Lord made me understand that a leader has the responsibility of going before the followers-clearing paths, encountering the danger that lurks in hidden places along the way. He made me understand that followers can only see as clearing takes place. Based on that insight, the response of David's band of men wasn't strange. They were as sheep needing leadership. They were filled with fear. Sheep scatter at the sign of trouble. They were responding as is typical of sheep.

However, it was David's response as the impending king of the united kingdom of Israel that should be noted. He could have decided to distance himself from the band of men that had fallen into his care, but what would that have accomplished? David's destiny was that of a great leader. His response at a time such as this is what was being tested. So what would he do?

David's Decision

We are told that David encouraged himself. Encouraged himself at a time such as this? How? My guess is he remembered from prior experiences that his help came from God and that God does not respond to emotions. He would need to steady himself so that he could commune with God based on trust in Him and His promises. He would draw from his prior experiences when there was no one to encourage him, when there was no one to sing songs regarding his victories, no one to prophesy over him. He had received similar treatment before. He had been rejected and turned on after doing good deeds many times in the past. Actually, it had probably been the training needed for such a time as this.

Therefore, I can imagine that he might have begun speaking to himself—to the seat of his emotions as he remembered the words he had penned back in the Cave of Adullam: "Why art thou cast down, O my soul? And why are thou disquieted in me?" (Psalm 42:5a). This might have steadied him so that he could think rather than respond hysterically. He would continue to speak to his soul: "Hope thou in God: for I shall yet praise him for the help of His countenance" (Psalm 42:5b). Now he could recall what he had done in the face of trouble in the past. He had learned to seek direction from the Lord before engaging in any activity, so he turned to the Lord and inquired of him, "Shall I pursue—Shall I overtake them?" (1 Samuel 30:7—8). The Lord responded, "Go after them—you will catch them and recover the captives."

A Heart Tried by Fire

David and his men's finding after returning home is another example of a major interruption in life. David, thus far in his journey, during times of trouble, allowed his confidence in God to govern his responses to troublesome situations. Now, once again, an unexpected situation was confronting him. How would he respond? Would emotions or a heart that had been tried and tested govern his actions?

We must stay true to our calling even if we have to stand alone. We have been given the promise that God will never leave us or forsake us. Granted, sometimes we really struggle with that. God's silence and delay, as we see it, really presents a challenge in our lives. However, we must remember that is exactly what these situations and interruptions in life are all about—challenging our faith and commitment to stay with God no matter what. Paul, in the New Testament, states it this way: "Who shall separate us from the love of Christ?" He then goes on to put forth some familiar challenges that occur in life: Will tribulation, or distress, or persecution, or famine, or nakedness, or peril, or sword? (Romans 8:35)

It is during such times that our character, our faith, our confidence in God are being tried and perfected. It is often during such times that we are being prepared for something beyond what our eyes can see, our ears hear, or our hearts can imagine.

Point to Ponder

Pressure does not shape our hearts—it reveals them. When life collapses around us, like Ziklag in ashes, we often discover who we truly trust. David's strength came not from the people around him, but from the God within him. When emotions scream and fear rises, choose what David chose: encourage yourself in the Lord. In every test, God is not trying to break you—He is building the character needed for the victories ahead.

CHAPTER 24

A Different Set of Principles
1 Samuel 30:21—31

D avid and his men returned from the battle against the Amalekites with their families, everything their rival had stolen from them, and more. They now had an abundance of food and supplies. It is at such a time as this that Godly values instilled in our heart are needed.

God had called for David to be anointed as king. He had identified him as a man after His own heart. Therefore, God was putting in him those characteristics needed for success. But most importantly, God was instilling in him those characteristics that qualified him for such a distinction. God was writing a different set of principles on the table of his heart. These would be principles that would follow David all the days of his life. Godly wisdom would be needed to be effective as king over the united kingdom of Israel. Godly wisdom is said to be "pure, peaceable, gentle and easy to be entreated, full of mercy and good fruits, without partiality and without hypocrisy" (James 3:17). We could only know if David had acquired this type of wisdom by his actions.

Greed and Selfishness

Covetousness and idolatry have a common connection. It is known as greed. The term *covetousness* is defined as "desiring what belongs to someone else." Colossians 3:5 (GNB) also lets us know that greed is a form of idolatry. Certainly, we are aware that idolatry is the worship of idols. Idols may be anything, or any person, to which excessive devotion, adoration, or reverence are given. Greed and selfishness might have given David to only show concern for his own at this point—me and mine only. Instead, following the adage "Charity begins at home," he first took care of affairs at home—among his own band of men. Afterward, he seized the opportunity to reach beyond his own camp.

All Needed, All Important

Two hundred of David's band of men had been too weak to go out to battle. Therefore, they had been left behind to keep the camp. The remaining four hundred men that went to battle felt the task of keeping the camp was not important to their overall success. Isn't that interesting? These men—the warriors—seemed to view what these men had done much like David's elder brother viewed him and his responsibility when watching his father's. sheep. Therefore, their attitude was that these men should have no part in the bounty. They wanted to only return their families to them and send them away. Sadly, the attitude of David's brother and these men yet prevails today. Individuals, for some reason, seem to think the finished product they get to enjoy happens spontaneously. Every endeavor, and I do mean every *successful* endeavor, requires the labor of many individuals behind the scene.

David intervened and stopped what could have become a division among the men and trouble in the camp. He said "not so" to their proposed plan. He reminded them of the source of their victory. It wasn't because they were such great warriors or superior to their fellow warriors. Rather, it was the Lord who had given them the great bounty and preserved and delivered them from their enemy, the Amalekites. David's action validated the importance of every individual's contribution. It is stated this way in New Testament: "Nay much more those members of the body, which seem to be more feeble, are necessary" (1 Corinthians 12:22).

David's statement also acknowledged loud and clear that he recognized the source of his help. I detect a level of frustration with these men in that he asked the instigator, "Who will listen to you in this matter?" Then he settled the dispute. Those that went to battle and those that stayed behind to keep the camp would receive the same portion.

Helping Hands Remembered

There had been times that David and his men existed entirely on what they could gather in the fields and from those that befriended them. He now had plenty. He now seized the opportunity to show concern for others beyond his own family and camp. He did not forget those who helped them when they were impoverished. David's next act is also worthy of emphasis. He would show appreciation to those who had not abandoned him during his time of troubles. The importance of experiences has been emphasized throughout this book. Maybe it was the remembrance of his troublesome encounters that now motivated him. Surely he remembered his expectation of Nabal, how he thought Nabal would eagerly share his bounty in appreciation for acts of kindness extended to his men. David would not now be a hypocrite. Then what would be the difference in his actions and those of Nabal's? How could he have felt justified in being upset with Nabal for withholding an expression of kindness and now do the same? Remember, we are warned to judge not, lest we be judged (Matthew 7:1). We will be held to the standards (judgment) we render to others.

There had been times that David and his men existed entirely on what they could gather in the fields and from those that befriended them.

He now had plenty. He now seized the opportunity to show concern for others beyond his own family and camp. He did not forget those who helped them when they were impoverished.

Point to Ponder

Blessing is not just measured by what we gain, but by how we respond once we have it. After victory, David chose generosity over greed and unity over division—revealing a heart shaped by God, not by circumstance. When God prospers us, may we remember the source of every good gift and look for ways to honor Him through fairness, gratitude, and open-handed kindness.

CHAPTER 25

It Is a Promise
1 Samuel 30:21–31 (Addendum)

I can imagine that David wished he could have paid for the supplies they needed and even to have helped those that put their lives in danger to help him. However, he didn't have anything to give at the time. At some point, God provides the opportunity to return the kindness (pay it forward). It is not necessarily from the individual it was rendered. The manner you received it-payment in kind—is not necessarily what will be of great value to the one having addressed your need. This principle was demonstrated by the early church. Individuals with abundance sold and gave. There was sharing so that there was balance between those that had much and those that had little. People at times give out of their need. However, often they give from their abundance. It should not be mistakenly thought that only certain individuals have needs or that you could never have anything to offer. They may not have need of that which they gave. An abundance of things may even make some feel they have no need. I say with assurance everybody, now or at some point, will have a need.

My personal experience is that what I have to offer becomes what they need. What one has in abundance becomes the answer to my need and vice versa. Understanding of this principle helps me receive the help God sends in the time of my need with a heartfelt thank-you and the personal assurance that their kindness will be returned.

A Lesson in Receiving

Until a few years ago, I would send thank-you cards to individuals for kindnesses extended to me. I would close them out by saying, "I pray God will return to you what you have given to me." One day, as I started to pen to a card this statement, the Holy Spirit brought my attention to Luke 38. There, it says, "Give and it shall be given." Suddenly, I realized I need not pray that it be returned. It shall be! That is a promise, a sure thing, a fact what is given will be given in return (good or bad). What a revelation. Now I simply write, "I thank God for returning to you the kindness you've extended to me."

Point to Ponder

Every act of kindness is a seed God never forgets. We may not always be able to repay those who help us, but God promises that what is given—whether out of abundance or need—will return in His perfect way and timing. When we learn to receive help with gratitude and trust His promise of "give, and it shall be given," we discover that generosity is never lost. In God's hands, it always finds its way back.

CHAPTER 26

The Pursuit Ends
1 Samuel 31–2 Samuel 1:1—27

T here are times in life that it seems as though all efforts to do right are for naught. It seems that the individuals engaged in evil activities prosper and enjoy successes that seem to elude those endeavoring to live Godly. The ability to endure and stay faithful to Christian principles can become extremely challenging when observing such seeming injustices in life. Delayed change and eyes focused on the prosperity of the workers of wickedness have resulted in many individuals being drawn away from prior oaths of trust and faithful continuance in the things of God. Sadly, they usually give up right at the point of their breakthrough.

A study of the word of God regarding the fate of the wicked provides understanding of how falling prey to this trap could take place. In fact, it is the design of the enemy to get us to focus on and long for things that perish, become exhausted from the cares of life and his wicked devices launched toward us. A number of individuals in Scripture have been plagued by this same dilemma. Thankfully, many of them were able to maintain their belief that God would vindicate them. Although time would and does oftentimes seem long, God will vindicate.

David was one of those individuals. Saul had, for a long time, seemed to be prospering in his evil ways. He had plotted and schemed against David, but he had not succeeded in any of his efforts. God had always provided a way of escape for David: "There has no temptation that has come upon you that God will not provide strength to endure or a way of escape" (1 Corinthians 10:13).

A rule of thumb I've adapted in times like these is that if God has not delivered me out of it, there is a purpose for the situation persisting. I begin to consider my ways. Maybe God is allowing the situation so that a condition in my heart will be revealed so it can be dealt with.

Afterward, I draw encouragement from these words: "Evildoers shall be cut off: but those that wait upon the Lord, they shall inherit the earth. For yet for a little while, the wicked shall not be: yea, thou shalt diligently consider his place, and it shall not be" (Psalm 37:9—10). I have seen the fulfillment of this admonition on numerous occasions.

The End Is Nigh

Unknown to David, his stay away from his own country was drawing to an end. He was off fighting Israel's enemy, the Amalekites, at the same time Saul was off fighting the Philistines. Yes, David was engaged in performing the tasks that had resulted in God withdrawing His spirit from Saul. Remember, Saul disobeyed God's instructions to destroy the Amalekites and everything that pertained to them.

Saul, on the other hand, was now compelled to go to battle against the Philistines without the protective arm of the Lord. The predicament he found himself in was all his own making. It was the fruit of allowing the evil inside his heart to persist. The battle would mark the end of his evil activities. He would not return from that battle. He and three of his sons, including Jonathan, were killed. That was one of the scenarios that David had spoken regarding Saul's fate: "He shall descend into battle and perish" (1 Samuel 26:10). David had trusted God to fight his battle. Saul had been killed in battle against the Philistines.

Reputation Protected

I love the scripture that says, "A man's heart deviseth his way, but the Lord directeth his steps" (Proverbs 16:9). The result is what many have already come to know by way of experience—that is, the Lord, at times, will interrupt our plans, causing the need for another course of action. Many times such occurrences meet with mumbling, complaining, discouragement, and sadness. Often it causes confusion. Regardless of our initial response, we often, at a later date, arrive at the realization that our plans were interrupted for our good even to the saving of our lives.

Such was the case with the Philistines not allowing David and his men to accompany them into battle against Israel. We already saw that David and his army were needed by their families back at Ziklag. Now we see that it also provided David an alibi and protection from evil communications, false accusations, and further trouble with regard to Saul's death.

Specifically, news of Saul's and Jonathan's deaths came to David three days after he had returned from the battle at Ziklag. What if the Philistines had allowed him to accompany them into battle rather than insisting that he return to Ziklag? David might have been falsely accused of killing Saul on the battlefield. Instead, to the very end, his hands remained clean with regard to King Saul. Likewise, in spite of the anguish and cruel treatment inflicted upon him by Saul, it appears his heart had remained pure. Such behavior continued as he did not take pleasure in the news. David appeared to sincerely mourn their deaths.

Mourn—Do Not Rejoice

It is not strange that our desire for our enemy while we are being mistreated is that they be cut off. Therefore, mourn! You might be thinking, *Why wouldn't David be rejoicing?* The answer is in remembering that God had identified David as a man after His own heart. Therefore, we are seeing evidence of David's behavior being in line with God's character. Specifically, Jesus gave the command to love our enemies and pray for them that despitefully use us (Luke 6:28). Now, as with all His commands, there is purpose. I've come to experience that the purpose in obeying this particular command is that it makes it possible to obey another of His commands: "Do not rejoice when your enemy falls, and do not let your heart be glad when he stumbles" (Proverbs 24:17). Yes, it is in the Bible. Furthermore, to do otherwise could result in bringing trouble upon ourselves. We are admonished of the consequences of this expected tendency: "He who is glad at calamity will not go unpunished" (Proverbs 17:5b) and "Lest the Lord see it, and it displease Him and He turn away his wrath from him" (Proverbs 24:18).

David's sincerity was further expressed after he tore his clothes, mourned, wept, and fasted. His actions were as though delivering King Saul's and his friend Jonathan's eulogies. David paid tribute, expressed a sense of loss, and spoke of their unique achievements in a poem. He further gave instructions that their skill with the bow be taught to the nation. That action would help the nation undergo the process of grieving their loss in a healthy manner. They were to focus on King Saul's and Jonathan's contributions while alive rather than dwelling on the sorrow or sense of loss they might have been experiencing.

Notice what David did not do. He did not use the occasion to broadcast any expressions of bitterness nor vengefulness toward Saul. Instead, he focused attention on Saul's contributions to the nation in a manner that would be lasting and spread afar off. That is a lesson we would do well to embrace. We are not to focus on the bad of the deceased. Instead, we are to extol the good that can be accredited to a person's life.

It Comes Together

The command to love our enemies does not refer to an emotional attachment. Instead, it means to have a genuine concern for them. That stands to reason because we are admonished to put on the mind of Christ. His desire is that none would perish but all come to repentance. So what follows when we are concerned about an individual or situation? Hopefully, we pray as we are commanded. During the span of time that we are praying for the individual, a twofold change occurs.

SURPRISE! The first change often occurs within our heart. Our hurt and desire for our enemy's demise begin to fade. Those crippling emotions of hatred, bitterness, desire for revenge, and the like are replaced with feelings of sadness for their condition and a heartfelt longing for their deliverance, healing, and salvation. We get delivered and healed when we pray for our enemy. Our desired blessings are often released as well, much like it happened with Job. He was the individual in the Old Testament that was falsely accused by his friends of suffering multiple hardships and a prolonged illness because of having sinned. Job obeyed God's command to pray for his accusers. He then received more in his latter days of life than he had in the beginning (Job 42:10).

Second, if we are praying and earnestly desiring God's best (deliverance, healing, and salvation) for our enemy, then news of anything contrariwise will bring the same reaction as David's. He mourned rather than rejoiced over the misfortune of his enemy.

Point to Ponder

When it seems the wicked prosper and justice takes too long, remember: God's timetable is never late. He sees every struggle, every tear, and every act of faithfulness. Like David, we are called not to rejoice in the downfall of others, but to trust the God who judges righteously. As we keep our hearts pure and our prayers sincere—even for those who hurt us—we discover that God is working both in our circumstances and within us. Stay faithful... your breakthrough may be nearer than you think.

CHAPTER 27

Now Where Do I Go?
2 Samuel 2:1—7

David had sworn before escaping to the Philistine territory not to touch God's anointed, King Saul. He had remained there out of Saul's reach for sixteen months. Now that King Saul was dead, there was no need to stay there any longer. He could now go back to be with his own people, the Israelites. But would it be as simple as packing up and returning? Returning to what and where exactly? Would his countrymen, the Israelites, be convinced that he had not gone over to the side of their enemy, the Philistines?

David asked the Lord, "Shall I go up into any of the cities of Judah?"

The Lord replied, "Go up."

David then asked, "Where shall I go up?"

God instructed him to go to Hebron. Notice how David was careful to get specific directions from the Lord. He appeared to have no problem asking God one question after another. He wanted clarity. He wanted to do nothing except what was in line with God's plan for his life. Again, he would not presume to know what was to happen next.

Why Hebron?

Why would God tell David to go there? First, we see that Hebron was a haven of refuge. It was a city where men such those that had followed David would be able to settle. They had endured the hardships of being away from home with David. Certainly, David would not leave them behind now.

Second, Hebron was a city in Judah. David was also from a city among the tribe of Judah. The implication would be that he might have had friends there. The Bible speaks of casting your bread upon the waters followed by the promise of it returning. The symbolism here is that bread (meaning grain) would be cast upon water during high tides, allowing it to take root during low tides later to produce a harvest. David had cast much bread upon the waters in the form of kindnesses during his time in exile. The tribe of Judah had been a recipient on a number of occasions. It was enemies of their cities that David and his men had warred against from Ziklag. Afterward, he would restore unto them that which had been taken. He had done the same upon returning to Ziklag from the camp of the Amalekites: "He sent of the spoil to the elders of Judah and his friends saying, behold a present for you from the spoil of the enemies of the Lord" (1 Samuel 30:26).

The third possibility was that the tribe of Judah often stood alone. They were accustomed to acting independently from Israel.

Prophecy Fulfilled

In light of the aforementioned facts, what happened next is not strange. Upon arriving in Hebron, the men of Judah came and anointed David king over the house of Judah. They acted on their own behalf, separate from Israel. Thereby, their decision to anoint David as their king caused the once united kingdom of Israel to be split.

Finally, David would ascend to the office for which he had previously been anointed. But would he? Let's not be hasty. Let's not try to make the situation be the fulfillment of the prophecy.

David had been anointed to reign over the united kingdom of Israel the northern and southern tribes, not Judah alone. David was yet journeying toward the position God had sent his servant Samuel to anoint him to occupy many years earlier.

We so often get partial instructions and feel that we can take the project from that point. However, experience has made me realize I should not move hastily. I have learned it is okay to ask God and wait for further clarity and specifications: "Acknowledge God in all your ways and He will direct your paths" (Proverbs 3:6). God wants us to trust and obey Him. Asking Him for clarity is not an indication of distrust. In fact, it is with clarity that we are able to obey and avoid a number of false starts, costly mistakes, and even situations that take a long time and much prayer to get out of. He that believes will not make haste (Isaiah 28:16b) but waits God's time for the accomplishment of His promises. David would serve as the king of Judah from Hebron for the next seven and half years. The prophecy was partially fulfilled at this time.

Point to Ponder

When life seems uncertain and the next step unclear, remember David's example: seek God's guidance with patience and precision. Partial instructions are not a license to rush ahead; clarity comes from waiting on the Lord. Trust Him to direct your path, and step confidently only when He provides the full picture. Obedience and patience today pave the way for the fulfillment of God's promises tomorrow.

CHAPTER 28

Another Attempt to Stop God's Plan
2 Samuel 2:8–2 Samuel 4:1—12

I am sure you have had the experience of getting through one tough situation to immediately be faced with another. How do you respond when that happens? Do you fall into despair, depression, and feelings of just wanting to throw in the towel and give up on life? If so, I want you to know you're not alone in experiencing one fiery trial after another at times. It is a fact that we will be faced with troubles and afflictions at various times. Isn't it interesting that the Bible tells us they come for a purpose? It is often after we've come through the situation sometimes far down the road that we come to realize how the experiences of that situation had prepared us for the next, and yet each time we are tempted to repeat the woe-is-me dialogue—"Will this ever pass? Why me?"

God's Wisdom

I am amazed at the long-suffering and restraint of our Heavenly Father toward us. We human beings, and especially parents, are quick to jump in and rescue our children and loved ones when they are in trouble, most times without asking the Lord what He would have us do. Oftentimes we are circumventing their growth, deliverance, and even maturity. Yes, it hurts to see anyone we love hurting. Think of it in this light: the Lord loves us, but He doesn't always immediately pull us out of adverse situations. He is, however, always with us as we journey through them. It is often in the midst of the troublesome situation that we become equipped for success in life. Or at the very least, we are being prepared for the next leg of the journey to meet up with our destiny. You might need to pause, reread, and even think on that statement again. It is not an easy fact to embrace.

Trouble Will Arise

Trouble and various trials are a part of life's journey. Our focus, however, is not to fixate on the troublesome situation but rather, trust God to help us in our times of trouble. We should reflect on the many times in the past that He extended mercy, proved Himself faithful, commanded man to show us favor, and even worked miracles on our behalf during hardships. Certainly, as He did it before, He will do it again. David's previous experiences made him know these facts about God. He was confident that the same God that had been with him before in times of trouble would be with him again.

Trouble Has a Purpose

It was good for me to be afflicted so that I might learn your decrees (Psalm 119:71). For our slight momentary affliction is preparing for us an eternal weight of glory beyond all comparison (2 Corinthians 4:17). So it was with David as he journeyed toward the position of king over the united kingdom of Israel-Judah and Israel. He had many successes behind him. He had come a long way, but there was yet another roadblock.

One of Saul's younger sons, Ish-bosheth, was yet alive. He had no personal aspirations or qualifications to be king. However, being Saul's son, he would be in line to assume the position.

His father's army commander influenced him to assume the position of king over Israel. Why would this commander do this, you might ask. The answer is not explicitly stated. However, maybe you could venture a guess once I tell you the name of this individual. He was Abner-yes, the same Abner that David scolded for allowing an outsider (namely himself) to get close enough to kill Saul while he slept (1 Samuel 26:13 —— 16).

David had commended Abner for being a valiant man and said there was none as capable as he was, but he had fallen down on the job. David had entered the camp without detection and taken the king's spear and cruse of water. He then voiced all these things from a distance in the hearing of King Saul and his company. Just maybe, Abner had logged the incident into his memory bank. Maybe he was now using this occasion to retaliate. In the following years, there was war between the two—the house of David versus the house of Saul. During this time, David grew stronger and stronger, while the house of Saul grew weaker and weaker.

Deliverance Will Come

Many are the afflictions of the righteous, but the Lord delivers him out of them all (Psalm 34:19). When the purpose of the trouble is accomplished, then God causes it to come to an end. The means by which this deliverance is accomplished is often when least expected through a means never anticipated. Jesus's response to a group of religious leaders who questioned the miracle performed on behalf of a blind and deaf man was, "Every kingdom divided against itself will be ruined, and every city or household divided against itself will not stand" (Matthew 12:25). We can see the application of that truth in what happened on David's behalf next.

A House Divided

Deliverance was accomplished through a rift that occurred between Saul's son and his army commander,

Abner. The kingdom began experiencing division from within. Initially, Abner had rallied the tribes to divide the kingdom—Judah against Israel. Now he went about to undo what he had done previously. He went about rallying Israel to make David their king. He reminded the people of their prior desire for David to be their king. He also rehearsed God's saying in their ears. Abner, previously David's enemy, was now campaigning for David. Afterward, he desired to enter into a league with David. As he returned from a meeting with David, he was killed. Later, Saul's son, Ish-bosheth, king of Israel, was also killed by men of his kingdom while he lay upon his bed.

God promises to fight our battles if we just sit still. Once again, this sure promise was demonstrated in David's life. Another of his enemies was removed. It happened, and once again, David had clean hands with regard to the matter.

Point to Ponder

Trials often arrive one after another, testing our patience, faith, and trust in God. Yet, just as David experienced, God's timing is perfect—He works behind the scenes, orchestrating deliverance and victory in ways we may never expect. Trust Him in the waiting, remain faithful, and remember: God fights your battles while keeping your hands clean.

CHAPTER 29

Established King, Exalted Kingdom
2 Samuel 5:1—25

The men of Israel found their way to David after the death of King Ish-bosheth. They said unto David, "We are thy bone and thy flesh. Also in time past, when Saul was king over us, you were the one who led out and brought them in: and the Lord said, 'You shall shepherd my people Israel, and be ruler over Israel" (2 Samuel 5:1 — 2). Then they anointed him king over Israel. David was now king over Judah and Israel—all of the united kingdom of Israel. Now he was in the office for which he had been anointed as a youth. It had been a number of years since he had been called from the sheep pasture to stand before Samuel the prophet to be anointed for this position.

David was now far into his thirties. He was around the age of seventeen when he fought and killed Goliath. I can only imagine what he might have thought as he recounted the various experiences he encountered along the way to this position in his life. Certainly, he would have never imagined they were a part of his preparation for the task ahead.

Nevertheless, throughout the journey, he continued to do what he must to survive. He exercised restraint in the face of opportunities to vindicate himself. He never tried to elevate himself or usurp the authority of the one that seemed to stand in his way. He exercised great patience in waiting to see what God would do for him. We are told in Isaiah 55 that God's word will accomplish what it was sent out to do. The fulfillment of David's destiny had unfolded gradually. At God's appointed time, the word He had spoken through the prophet Samuel several years earlier came to pass. It happened gradually, but it came to pass.

First Order of Business

The goal was to have a united kingdom—Israel. David was wise enough to know that popularity wasn't sufficient to produce unity. Nor was it something he could trust to ensure his position as king. He was now king over both the northern and southern kingdoms—all of Israel. But he yet had a potential problem. Where would he establish the capital to avoid an uprising between the two kingdoms? It could not be located too far north, nor could it be too far south.

Between Judea and the larger part of the kingdom of Saul (Israel) lay a well-fortified city called Jerusalem. It was not identified with the southern tribes like Hebron nor with the northern state of Israel. It was neutral ground. However, it was yet occupied by the Canaanites and known as Jebus (1 Chronicles 11:4). The Israelites had failed to conquer it when taking possession of the land God had given them. David attacked and acquired it as his personal territory. It became known as the city of David and the solution to David's latest dilemma. The capital would be located in Jerusalem.

Twice an Enemy

Abner had pressed Israel to anoint David as their king by reminding them of what God had spoken concerning David: "By the hand of my servant David I will save my people Israel out of the hands of the Philistines; and out of the hand of all their enemies" (2 Samuel 3:18). Once again, the Philistines surfaced for battle against the united kingdom of Israel. This time they came because they heard David had been anointed as their king. Likewise, David heard they had come to seek him. David did as it had been his custom. He asked the Lord two questions: "Shall I go up to the Philistines?" and "Will You deliver them into my hands?" The Lord responded with a yes in both instances. The battle took the form of two parts. In both instances, the Philistines were defeated as David obeyed the command of the Lord.

Point to Ponder

God's timing is perfect, and His plans unfold gradually. Like David, we are often being prepared for positions, purposes, and victories that seem distant. Patience, obedience, and trust in His guidance allow God's promises to be fulfilled in their season, and when we act in alignment with His Word, success comes as a result of His faithfulness, not our haste.

CHAPTER 30

A Place for God's Presence
2 Samuel 6:1—23

During his journey, David had probably learned that obstacles were only opportunities in his life for God to show up and prove Himself strong and mighty on his behalf. He would probably also realize that the man he had now become had surfaced during times of hardships. He had faced and overcome obstacles throughout his entire life.

Military Brilliance

The real show of David's military brilliance can be seen in the way he faced this new obstacle. He had started this journey trusting in the Lord for victory over his enemies—animal and man. That practice had not changed throughout his entire journey. Why would it change now? Would he now change because he had arrived at this high and lofty position? Would he now be foolish enough to become ensnared by the appearance of all the people being on his side? His next move reveals that he had also acquired Godly wisdom during his journey. He was not quick to forget his wilderness experiences. Specifically, he might have been recalling the incident at Ziklag. There, the people having previously run to him for direction and protection turned and talked about stoning him.

A Narrow Scope

Equally, it seems to indicate he had not forgotten who had remained on his side. He was fully aware of the fact that it was the Lord that bought him victory after victory. He would not now rise up and forget the Lord. He probably also had not forgotten that Saul's downfall escalated because he continued to disobey God. The result was a breach in his relationship with the man of God, Samuel the prophet, and killing the priest at Nob. There had been a connection between victories enjoyed and the political being in line with the religious. So now he would bring the ark of God home. Scripture tells us the ark (God's presence) had been gone all through Saul's reign. It is no wonder Saul himself spiraled downward to the point of utter demise. His focus on the kingdom and securing it for his son was too narrow in scope. It was self—centered and not God—focused. It resulted in the demise of both himself and three of his sons.

Small Beginnings

David, on the other hand, recognized that his victories and protection during his days of striving against his enemies had come from a source greater than himself. He had learned early in life (watching the sheep) and had become unshakably convinced of this fact while making his home in the woods, caves, and wilderness. The times he had spent in isolation and solitary places were not to be despised. They were only the days of small beginnings. They had purpose. That purpose might have been as he penned in Psalm 23: "Yea though I walk through the valley." Indeed, David had walked it out with full assurance that God's presence (reliance on God) was the key to his success.

Therefore, now he had responsibility for far more than the initial six hundred men. Therefore, his attention and priority were to bring God's presence back—to bring the Ark of the Covenant home. He would set it up in Jerusalem. The story of David's efforts to accomplish this feat are told in the 2 Samuel 6 and the 1 Chronicles 13—14. This would put the seal on his position. It also emphasized the fact that he was a man after God's heart—always seeking to know and doing the will of God.

Point to Ponder

True success begins and endures when God's presence is at the center of our lives. Like David, our victories are not just the result of skill or strategy, but of faithfully acknowledging God, learning from past trials, and making Him the priority in every step we take.

CHAPTER 31

Hindsight

Have you ever wondered how flowers, such as crocus, daffodils, tulips, and other early —— spring —— blooming flowers, survive harsh winter conditions to lavish us with their beauty at the very first sign of spring? Did you know the bulbs from which these flowers emerge are to be planted in the fall? They actually need to be in the ground to undergo the cold winter conditions to shower us with their beauty come spring and summer. It is during the winter months that they acquire their root growth before having to withstand dry conditions the following summer. Deeper, better established roots are a large factor in determining how well a plant tolerates drought.

It is likewise in our lives. The deeper our trust in the Lord has been established before faced with extreme difficulties, the more certain we will be able to stand during hard times. Acquiring this trust requires more than intellectual knowledge. Like the spring-flowering bulbs, our lives must undergo winter seasons. These are the times our faith is tried, our character tested, and we gain unshakeable trust in God. The Old Testament prophet Jeremiah expressed it this way: "Blessed is the man that trusts in the Lord and whose hope is in the Lord. For he shall be like a tree planted by the waters, which spreads out its roots by the river, and will not fear when heat comes, but its leaf will be green; and will not be anxious in the year of drought, nor will cease from yielding fruit" (Jeremiah 17:7—8).

Entering into the position we have been called does not happen overnight. Although to the public, it often seems that way. The reason is they were not privy to the maturing processes that were taking place beforehand. God doesn't have to plan ahead. He has already been ahead. He now orchestrates our steps through various experiences of life to bring us to that expected end He has in mind for us. Remember, He sees the end from the beginning.

The prophet Samuel obeyed God. He had anointed David for the office of king over the nation of Israel. The words the prophet spoke would not be fulfilled for years. However, David's every experience in life along the way was preparing him for fulfillment of that God——inspired word.

There is an adage that says "hindsight is 20/20 vision." The meaning is that we can see perfectly when looking back (hindsight) on a situation.

We can now look back and see the importance of the situations encountered by David. Prior to now, we could only see interruptions that seemed unfair and without any connection to his destiny. Throughout this journey, many might have questioned why David would be brought out of the sheep pasture, where he was experiencing peace and God's presence, to enter the life of someone that would bring him so much grief. So cruel, it seems!

David's gift was that of a warrior. He would be fighting the Lord's battles. The position in which he was anointed to carry it out was as king of the united kingdom of Israel. God had chosen him, describing him as a man after His (God's) heart. David would seek to fulfill the desires of God in whatever he would do. He had to have unshakeable faith in God. Furthermore, he would demonstrate characteristics consistent with those of God's. It would be through his various experiences that such characteristics would be developed and perfected.

David had come from the secluded sheep's pastures with absolute confidence that he could depend on the Lord to always help him, "The Lord who delivered me from the paw of a lion and the paw of a bear will deliver me from the hand of this Philistine." That confidence was developed while doing a job looked down upon and despised by many.

He was summoned to the palace under the pretense of being there to play his harp for King Saul. His gift of music made room for him. He would see and be seen in the place where his calling was to take him. However, he was only to pass through at this time.

An abrupt departure was necessary. The people had begun to exalt David above Saul. This was a nation of people that held no allegiance to anyone—not even God. Certainly, their behavior would not be any different toward an earthly leader. Soon they would begin to look to David as their leader rather than Saul. Any healthy organization can only have one leader at a time. Therefore, David couldn't stay in the palace while Saul reigned.

"Nay, but we will have a king over us; that we also may be like all the nations; and that our king may judge us, and go out before us, and fight our battles" (1 Samuel 8:19b, 20). David's qualities as a warrior, the only quality that the people wanted, had been demonstrated. God was yet the one to provide victory over their enemies. He would do it through a servant that would consistently seek, hear, and obey His voice.

Upon Saul's death, David had no further need to remain in the wilderness. God directed him to go to Hebron. There, the people anointed him to be king over the two southern tribes of Judah. It was only partial fulfillment of what God had spoken because of another interruption. This one lasted for seven and half years. I believe its purpose can be gleaned from the statement "David grew stronger and stronger" (2 Samuel 3:1). I dare believe the reference was to a matter greater than his military capacity. He had transitioned from watching sheep in the field to leading six hundred men on war campaigns in the wilderness. This interruption would provide him time to settle into the position of king over a multitude of people. At the proper time, he would be ready to take responsibility of the additional ten northern tribes of Israel. Maturity and confidence comes with time.

The confidence he possessed coming out of the sheep pastures could only be rivaled by the wisdom, foresight, and ease through which he forged ahead to establish a place of worship and to bring the Ark of the Covenant home after becoming king of the united kingdom of Israel. It was the by-product of the many sad, unfair, and often unexpected experiences he encountered as he journeyed from the lowly despised position of shepherd boy in the remote city of Bethlehem to finally reign as king of a great nation from the capital city Jerusalem.

Point to Ponder

Just as spring flowers bloom after the harshness of winter, our lives are shaped and strengthened through seasons of trial and waiting. The challenges we endure prepare us for the fullness of God's plan, cultivating roots of faith and trust that cannot be shaken when we finally step into our destiny.

CHAPTER 32

Pause

At this juncture in David's life, we take a moment to pause. Stopping here is by no means a suggestion that all would go well in the future. As with all our lives, he would continue to be faced with many trials and temptations. Some he would pass with flying colors, others he would fail miserably. Yet down through the years, he has continued to be mentioned time and time again in sermons, referenced and quoted in times of sadness, grief, betrayal, lonely hours, and despair. He is best known for his success as a warrior and as a religious poet. His life was marked by a great number of interruptions during his journey from following after sheep in the fields to be king over the united kingdom of Israel. They all contributed to qualifying him as the person God had called a man after His heart.

These facts have been penned to encourage and provoke us to forever remember that "our light affliction which is but for a moment; works for us a far more exceeding and eternal weight of glory" (2 Corinthians 4:17). God is able to take that which seems to be meant for bad and turn it around. Thereby, the prophet Isaiah exhorts us to wait upon the Lord. We will be rewarded with renewed strength and the ability to mount up as on wings of eagles. Additionally, we will be able to run and not faint; walk and not be weary (Isaiah 40:31).

Therefore, if the life you had planned has suddenly been interrupted; if faced with divorce, death, job loss, or one of the many other unforeseen circumstances; if anointed and gifted in song, spiritual dance, prophecy, praise dancer, preacher, or teacher and such but not being acknowledged; if, at this moment, you are discouraged and in total despair, be encouraged.

God has a plan for each of our lives. His plan is not to destroy or withhold any good thing from us. He watches over His plan to perform it. He has an expected end in mind for each of us. Stay with the process and let patience have her perfect work. She will leave you wanting for nothing. God's timing is always right and never late. With God, nothing is wasted and nothing lost. He knows the way we should take. Should we stray off course, He is ever present to redirect our steps.

Final Reflection—A Life in God's Hands

David's journey from shepherd boy to king reminds us that life's interruptions, trials, and delays are not obstacles but instruments in God's hands to shape, refine, and prepare us for our destiny. Every setback, every period of waiting, and every challenge was part of a divine process to deepen his faith, strengthen his character, and root his trust in the Lord. Like David, we are called to trust the process, obey God faithfully, and acknowledge His presence in all we do. God's timing is perfect, nothing is wasted, and every step—even those that seem unfair or difficult—works together for a greater purpose. As we pause and reflect, let us remember: patience cultivates endurance, obedience produces blessing, and faith in God ensures that our ultimate victory is secure.

References

Allendale, Dan B. (1995). *The Wounded Heart.* Navpress, Colorado Springs, Colorado.

Bibles: King James; New International Version; Good News.

CBN.cm/biblestudy/responding to personal-prophecy.

Freeman, James M. (2012). *Handbook of Bible Manners and Customs.* Forgotten Books.

Great Bible Events of Bible Times. Doubleday.

King Jr., Martin Luther. *Strength to Love.* Fortress Press.

LaCour, Jean M. *Counseling the Codependent: A Christian Perspective Utilizing Temperament.*

Marin, William C. *These Were God's People: A Bible History.* The Southern Company, Nashville, Tennessee.

Maxwell, John C. *The 21 Irrefutable Laws of Leadership.* Nelson.

Stalking Resource Center-The National Center for Victims of Crime-www. NCVC.org/src-The Use of Technology to Stalk-DVD and Discussion Guide.

Thoele, Sue Patton. *The Courage to Be Yourself A Woman's Guide to Emotional Strength and Self-Esteem.* Conari Press.

Warren, Rick. *The Purpose Driven Life.* Zondervan.

Truthor Tradition.com. Things to Consider When Receiving a Prophecy.

http://bibleworld.com/Patmos.

http://www.sunset.com/garden/flowers-plants/fall-planting-guide.

http://bible-archaeology.info/bible_city_hebron.htm.

www.charactercounts.org/sixpillars.html.

www.Jewishencyclopedia.com.

www.psychologytoday.com.

www.ingramcontent.com/pod-product-compliance
Lightning Source LLC
Chambersburg PA
CBHW051216120626
46547CB00013B/1378